...ton
Diesel Depot
&
Locomotive
Duties

Steve Morris

© 2006 Steve Morris

ISBN 0-9552354-0-5
978-0-9552354-0-5

Design & typesetting by
Steve Morris

Printed by
WP Litho Ltd

Published by

Ty Mawr Publications
Holmes Chapel
Cheshire
UK
Email
sgw.morris@btinternet.com

May 1971and ex works Bristol Bath Road allocated Hymek 7044 waits its next turn of duty at the east end of Canton Servicing Shed along with class 46 number 184 (46047) and Canton allocated 7081.
7044 lasted another two years before being one of only a few Hymeks to be cut up by Birds of Long Marston. The demise of 7081 came only two months after this photograph was taken after catching fire at Bathampton in July 1971. Cutting came at Swindon works by the end of August 1972. 7081 spent less time in revenue earning service than any other Hymek.
Photo Ian Walmsley

Introduction

I started work at Canton Diesel depot during the summer of 1985 as a Senior Technical Officer (STO) or "general technical trouble-shooter". Fresh from University having been sponsored by British Railways through a degree in Mechanical Engineering, I started working on the Western Region Headquarters locomotive section during 1984. However, my main aim was to get a position on a depot, preferably one with an allocation of Diesel locomotives. Canton fitted the bill perfectly.

Within six months I was given the chance to act as a relief shift supervisor covering a person on long term sickness leave. This finally led to me getting my first permanent position on the railway as a Shift Engineer responsible for running the depot on a shift basis. I was completely inexperienced but willing to give it a go and, with the support of the other management and shop floor staff, I gained a huge amount of experience during the time spent in this role.

This publication attempts to provide a pictorial insight into Canton Diesel depot and some of the workings that its allocation of locomotives were responsible for covering during its 40 year history. The other part of the site, "The DMU" is not included and where I mention "Canton" this refers to the locomotive side of the depot unless otherwise stated.

With the introduction of Cost-effective Maintenance (CEM), multiskilling, Organisation for Quality (OfQ) and the resulting Sectorisation of the railway, my period at Canton was arguably the time of greatest change in the history of the depot.

Following my time at Canton, another significant change was to take place with privatisation, EWS taking control and the introduction of locomotive technology from the USA which would eventually play a large part in the closure of the depot.

I hope that the following pages bring back some memories to those who either visited the site as an enthusiast or were part of the professional team that kept a large proportion of the BR Diesel locomotive fleet operational for almost 40 years. In my opinion Canton was *the* premier Diesel depot in UK, but of course I am somewhat biased!

Finally, I hope that the facts presented here are accurate but would be quite happy to receive any corrections or general comments by email, my memory not being what it was!

Steve Morris
Holmes Chapel
January 2006

sgw.morris@btinternet.com

Acknowledgements

Thanks are due to a large number of people who have assisted with the preparation of this book but in particular to Colin Webb, Ian Walmsley, Andrew Skinner and Brian Penney who have provided valuable information and images which have enabled me to "fill in the gaps" in my knowledge. Last but not least to Sue, Matt and Jack for their support during the many hours I seem to have spent working on this project!

References

"The Allocation History of BR Diesels and Electrics" parts 1 to 5 by Roger Harris.

Credits

All photographs by the author unless otherwise stated.

Depot History

Cardiff Canton depot opened in June 1882 replacing a smaller shed situated a few miles east of Cardiff General station at Long Dyke. Coded CDF by the GWR the initial depot consisted of a 40 ft long six road shed. The facility was extended in 1897 with the addition of a "roundhouse" incorporating a 55 ft turntable with no less than 28 roads radiating off it.

Increasing demands on the depot resulted in the building of a lifting shed and new coaling stage in 1925. Final expansion under steam operation came in 1931 when a new 65 ft turntable was built at the west end of the facility.

Nationalisation in 1948 resulted in the depot being re-coded 86C under British Railways which was in turn replaced by 88A in 1960 then 86A in September 1963 and finally CF during May 1973.

Introduction of Diesel traction by the Western Region in the late 1950's resulted in the need for a number of chief Diesel depots on the region. Four were chosen, these being Cardiff Canton along with Plymouth Laira, Bristol Bath Road and London Old Oak Common. Dieselisation of the Cardiff Division commenced in 1962. A total of 26 Western and Hymek Diesel Hydraulics were allocated to 88A by the end of that year, the first of each type being D7022 in February and D1012 "Western Firebrand" in November along with class 37 D6742 on loan from Sheffield Darnall for clearance tests. Until full completion of the new Diesel depot at Canton these were maintained in part of the Servicing Shed and the recently opened DMU maintenance facility located on the same site, as well as at Godfrey Road depot Newport. The Divisional Diesel allocation had increased significantly by the summer of 1964 whilst Steam locomotives had reduced in number from 1,111 to 367 during the same period.

To enable the modernisation required to deal with Diesel traction, Canton was closed to Steam on Saturday the 8th September 1962 with the final Steam Locomotive to leave being Castle Class 5073 "Blenheim" to work the 19.30 Crewe TPO the following day.

Canton was demolished during the winter of 1962/63 and rebuilt by contractors Kyle Stewart at a cost of £1.32 Million on a 30 acre site. On the 10th of October 1963 the first section re-opened, a 270 ft long 3 road Servicing Shed which used parts of the original 1882 structure in its construction. Even though a large part of the depot was in use some months before, the official re-opening of the depot took place following the building of a new heavy maintenance facility on the site of the old roundhouse, with berths for 16 locomotives.

Presided over by the Rt Hon Lord Brecon, Minister of State for Welsh Affairs, this took place on Friday the 18th of September 1964 with Landore based class 47 D1756 ceremoniously breaking a ribbon whilst entering the new building which was to become known as the "Main Shed".

A new "Area Maintenance Engineer" (AME) organisation was set up early in 1965 and the first Depot Engineer to run Canton was Mr George Elliot who reported to the AME Cathays, Mr Jim McColl.

British Railways
Western Region

Opening Ceremony
Diesel Locomotive
Servicing and
Maintenance
Depot at Canton
Cardiff

by The Rt. Hon. Lord Brecon
Minister of State
(Welsh Affairs)
Friday
18 September 1964

Cardiff Canton Diesel depot was now officially on the map, the largest facility of its kind on the Western Region. The initial allocation numbered over 150 locomotives of classes 14/35/37/47 and 52 plus a solitary 08 shunter for training purposes, the remaining shunters being maintained at nearby Cathays depot at this time. This had risen to nearly 240 by the end of 1966 establishing Canton as one of the top 5 Diesel Traction Maintenance Depots (TMD's) in the UK. Initial traffic handled by the Canton allocation included various trip workings (class 14), passenger and freight duties (class 35 and 47), passenger (class 52) and freight (class 37).
An allocation snapshot for periods during the depot's history is provided in table 1.

Canton TMD closed on Sunday May the 30th 2004, nearly 40 years since opening, although the "Main Shed" had in fact ceased operation in the middle of February. The closure was due to several factors including the introduction of 3rd generation Diesel locomotives such as class 60/66/67 which were more reliable, required less routine maintenance and had superior haulage capability than the types they had replaced. This, combined with contraction in the coal and steel industry over several years plus of course Sprinterisation, which had effectively removed the need for any significant passenger locomotive servicing activity at the depot, and the writing was on the wall by the end of the 1990's. The final nail in the coffin came in the summer of 2003 when the Royal Mail cancelled its contract with EWS and transferred this business to road haulage and Air. This was a major blow to Canton which, along with Crewe Diesel depot, was a primary TMD for the Royal Mail traffic Diesel locomotive fleet as well as being responsible for the overhaul of a large proportion of the Royal Mail business locomotive hauled rolling stock.

Following closure, the remaining small allocation of class 08/09 shunters were transferred to Margam depot although in practise they are maintained at their various sites of operation by a mobile maintenance team.
The last mainline locomotives to leave the depot by rail were stored/withdrawn 37412/415/419/698 which were towed to Margam by 66032 on December 19th 2004. Apart from withdrawn shunters 08499/651/792/955/994 and 09008 this just left derelict 37509 which was finally cut up on site at the end of August 2005, the final mainline EWS Locomotive to "leave" the depot. The remaining EWS shunters left site in October 2005.
On a brighter note, in January 2005 the facility was purchased from EWS by Pullman Rail, a company that specialises in the overhaul of bogies and wheelsets fitted to a variety of rolling stock. Preserved class 26, 26038 is also being restored at the depot along with ex EWS shunter 08499 that has been returned to traffic by Pullman Rail to act as depot pilot for the wheel lathe. Whilst Canton is no longer host to a variety of locomotives it is still associated with and providing a service to the railway industry, and long may it continue ! Table 2 provides a chronology of the depot's history.   **Photos BR Western Region**

Plate 1
  18th September 1964 and Landore based D1756 (47162) with the appropriate year shown in the headcode box enters the
Main Shed from the west end breaking a ribbon on the way into 8 road to officially open *Canton Diesel depot.*
          Photo Ken Symons archive

Date	Allocation by Locomotive Class													Total
	08	09	14	25	35	37	46	47	52	56	60	66	67	
10/64	1	0	7	0	20	69	0	36	18	0	0	0	0	151
10/66	49	0	25	0	24	87	0	52	0	0	0	0	0	237
11/68	39	0	7	0	43	56	0	49	0	0	0	0	0	194
10/71	34	0	0	0	24	64	0	60	0	0	0	0	0	182
11/75	27	0	0	8	0	53	17	57	0	0	0	0	0	162
4/76	26	0	0	14	0	52	11	65	0	0	0	0	0	168
10/80	21	0	0	0	0	48	0	67	0	7	0	0	0	143
9/83	38	0	0	0	0	52	0	63	0	5	0	0	0	158
5/87	24	0	0	0	0	82	0	17	0	24	0	0	0	147
5/89	28	3	0	0	0	101	0	17	0	27	0	0	0	176
5/94	14	8	0	0	0	48	0	0	0	45	34	0	0	149
1/98	22	9	0	0	0	36	0	0	0	0	0	0	0	67*
11/01	28	12	0	0	0	4	0	0	0	1	21	46	30	142
1/04	22	12	0	0	0	9	0	0	0	0	19	47	30	139

*Note that the allocation and associated workload seems low due to central allocation of several complete fleets at Toton and Immingham during this period even though Canton continued to carry out heavy maintenance on them.

Table 1 above – Canton Diesel locomotive allocation snapshot

Table 2 right – Canton depot chronology

DATE	EVENT
June 1882	Steam depot opens under GWR – coded CDF
1897	Roundhouse built
1925	New Lift Shed and coaling stage introduced
1931	65ft turntable installed
1948	Nationalisation - British Railways Depot code 86C
1960	Re-coded 88A
February 1962	First mainline Diesel locomotive allocated Hymek class D7022
8/9/62	Depot closed to Steam traction
September 1963	Re-coded 86A
10/10/63	New Servicing Shed opened
18/9/64	Official re-opening of depot for Diesel traction
April 1966	Western Class allocation ended 14 remaining locomotives transferred to Laira
December 1970	Last of class 14 fleet leave depot – 9509 & 9519 to Kettering for cutting
19/12/72	Diesel Hydraulic locomotive allocation ended with withdrawal of Hymek 7098
May 1973	Re-coded CF under TOPS
1986/87	Sectorisation – Canton becomes a Freight Sector depot.
1/4/94	Rail Privatisation – Transrail operation commences
February 1996	EWS purchase of Transrail
June 2003	EWS loose Royal Mail contract
30/5/04	Depot closed by EWS
19/12/04	Stored mainline locomotives towed from depot leaving just 37509
January 2005	Depot purchased by Pullman Rail Ltd
August 2005	37509-Last EWS mainline locomotive remaining on the depot cut up on site

Canton Diesel depot

Canton Diesel depot was split into two specific sections, each with a particular function :

The Servicing Shed

The first part of the new depot to open in October 1963, this 3 road building was responsible for minor repairs and servicing. Normally, anything up to a B exam was carried out in the "SS" although on the odd occasion C exams were also undertaken here, particularly on refurbished class 37's due to a reduction in the C exam workload on these examples. However, any major items of work had to be carried out in the Heavy Lift Shop, this also included brake block renewal on class 37's and 50's due to the pits in the "SS" being too shallow to carry out this work.
An average 24 hour period in the mid 1980's would see approximately 40 locomotives pass through the Servicing Shed.
For the majority of its life, this part of the facility was manned over 3 shifts 24 hours a day throughout the year and dealt with locomotives from all over the country.

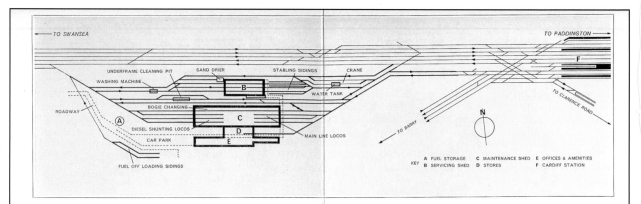

AN IMPORTANT PART OF WESTERN REGION'S MODERNISATION PROGRAMME continues to be the replacement of steam locomotives by diesel traction. Today sees a big step forward in this respect with the opening of the new *Diesel Locomotive Depot* at Canton, in Cardiff.

Occupying the site of the old steam locomotive depot, it virtually marks the end of the steam era in South Wales. Most of the old site has been cleared, and new, modern buildings have been erected. The new depot is the best-equipped of its kind in Europe. It can handle every type of diesel locomotive—electric and hydraulic also diesel multiple units.

Ten main line and six shunting diesels can be accommodated in the maintenance shed at any one time. And easy access to every part of the locomotive is made possible by means of permanent platforms between each set of tracks, and depressed floors below the rails.

Engine-changing is carried out in a two-track bay equipped with a 10-ton overhead crane; eight electric lifting jacks, each of 25-ton capacity, are provided for bogie-changing; there is also the latest type of locomotive weighing machine with two electronically operated load cell weighing units on the through road. A machine for tyre re-profiling is being installed in the adjacent carriage shed.

Daily or weekly servicing can be given to as many as nine locomotives simultaneously in the shed specially provided for this purpose.

Appearance as well as performance is important, too. And to ensure that the locomotives look their best when leaving the Depot, there is a washing machine controlled by photo electric cell equipment, and underframe cleaning facilities.

Storage space has been provided for 167,000 gallons of fuel oil.

At Canton, too, a highly specialised staff is always on hand to give the locomotives in their charge the best possible treatment. These technicians, engineers and other essential staff are accommodated adjacent to the Maintenance Shed. Welfare arrangements include an excellent mess-room, kitchen, cloakroom, drying room, locker room, washing facilities, and a first-aid room.

At this new Depot, you can see for yourself how Western Region is shaping up to British Railways' new forward-looking plans for top speed, top comfort in rail travel.

Extract from opening day brochure outlining the new depot facilities

The Heavy Lift Shop

Officially opened in September 1964 and commonly known as the "Main Shed", this part of the depot was responsible for all major routine maintenance (C/D/E/F exams) along with heavy repairs. B exams were also carried out here, particularly on class 56's which required a traction motor brush examination and even the odd A exam if the Servicing Shed workload was particularly high. It comprised 4 pitted roads with platforms, each capable of accommodating 2 mainline locomotives, 2 more with capacity for 3 shunters or a mainline loco and shunter along with a through road, one end of which was the "Jack Road", the other end with room for 2 more locomotives.

CLASS	EXAM					
	A	B	C	D	E	F
08/09	4 Weeks	4 Months	1 Year	2 Years	4 Years	
37/0-37/7	55	275	825	1650	4950	
37901-904 Mirrless	100	400	2000	4000		
37905-906 Ruston	80	400	1200	3600		7200
47	55	275	825	1650	4950	9900
56	60*	300*	1200	3600		7200

Intervals are in TOPS (operational) hours unless otherwise stated.
* Canton exam periodicity – lower than for class 56's allocated to other depot's
Table 3 – Exam periodicities - Year 1989

Plate 2
A view of the east end of the Main Shed and class 47's D1917 & D1902 sit outside 7 & 9 roads respectively in January 1966.
The height of this building compared to the Servicing Shed on the right hand side is evident in this photograph. This was as a result of the headroom required to carry out Diesel Hydraulic power unit changes within the shed, after all Canton was rebuilt as a "Hydraulic" locomotive maintenance facility even though it would lose its entire allocation of these just over six years after opening!
Both locomotives seen here were allocated to Canton at the time having been delivered from new in the final months of 1965. D1917 was finally to become ETH fitted 47818 and remains in use today under the ownership of Cotswold Rail. Meanwhile, D1902 was re-numbered 47226 in March 1974 and then 47384 following fitment of multiple working equipment at Tinsley depot in July 1994, before reverting back to "226" in November of 1995! Withdrawal came on February 2nd 1999 and sale to Fragonset Railways followed in March 2002. At the time of writing 47226 can be found stored at MOD Kineton.
Photo Brian Penney.

Following work carried out in the mid 1980's to focus on a more cost effective approach to locomotive maintenance, the so called CEM project, F and G exams were introduced to replace a proportion of the work that had previously been carried out at main works during Light and Intermediate overhauls. Canton was one of the depots nominated to carry out this work and as a result bogie and power unit "top end" overhaul became part of the depot's workload. A new 50 Tonne overhead crane replaced the original 40 Ton hoist at the west end of the shed as part of this initiative. As a result, Canton became one of a handful of freight sector depots with the ability to change power units, without having to borrow the depot breakdown crane.

Table 3 provides a breakdown of typical exam periodicities for the locomotive allocation at the end of the 1980's.

Facilities available within the Main Shed included a set of eight 25 Ton capacity jacks capable of lifting a complete locomotive for bogie removal to permit wheelset and traction motor changes, or for other repairs. In addition to this, there were 2 overhead cranes of capacity 3 & 10 Tons used for handling heavier items with the 10 Ton version having been capable of lifting the lighter weight power units associated with the Diesel Hydraulics initially allocated to the depot. A typical working day is shown in Table 4 which covers the depot stopped position for the 9th of May 1987.

Other facilities

Several other areas of the depot provided essential support to the maintenance activity. A ground wheel lathe was available, initially located adjacent to the DMU depot and latterly at the west end of the depot along with an underframe cleaning facility, also at the west end. For the majority of the depot's life these facilities were shared with the DMU side of the complex. A load bank was situated between the Servicing and Main Shed, this was used for tracing intermittent faults that were only seen under load as well as checking and setting up power units following major repair. In addition to this, lubricating oil and coolant sample analysis as well as fuel injector testing was carried out on site by depot staff as part of routine maintenance. Further support was provided by a team of plant maintenance staff responsible for the maintenance and repair of depot facilities. Last but not least, the all important stores department was responsible for provision of spare parts, lubricating oil, sand, brake blocks etc as well as managing provision of Diesel fuel, 167,000 gallons of which could be stored on the depot at any one time.

A diagram showing the depot layout and position on February 7th 2004, one week before closure of the Main Shed, is provided overleaf.

7 Road	9	11	13
37278	47225	37241	37797
B Exam / Fuel pump repairs	C Exam / Flat batteries / MOT to do	Brake blocks	C Exam / Brake blocks
37428	47624	47231	47560
Repaint for naming	E Exam / Main Generator flashover	C Exam	B Exam / B1/A5 / Piston & liner change
Spare Bogies	56040	08487	08787
Overhaul to progress	B Exam	D Exam / Brake blocks	C Exam & / Work arising
37147	47616		08589
No 5 Traction motor change	B Exam		A Exam

Jack Road	8	10	12
Underframe Clean	Lathe	Trial Run	Load Bank
56050 / C Exam	C480	37901	Empty

	C Road	B Road	Servicing Shed
Note : Shaded areas are covered "shed roads" 7/9/11/13 Main Shed roads face the East	56041- Waiting jacks – No 3/5 Traction motor / 37158 – Traction motor blower motor change / 47014 – Heat exchanger change / 37159 – 20% fuel dilution	37217 – Axle test / 37903 – B Exam / 47602 – Waiting material- governor / 37285 – D Exam progressing. Waiting material	37227 / 37229 / 47224 / 47297 / All A exam

Table 4 – Depot stopped position 9th May 1987

UFC

GWL

HOIST **Lathe**

08941
08576

Wagon
100081

37402   08957

Underframe
Cleaning
pit

ADB 965203
08955

SAND

12	10	8	7		5		3	2

ADRC 96714   09203
08792
                               08651

Main Shed

37422   37248
             67004   67001

**Load
Bank**

37685

DR 98913

DR 98963

**Servicing
Shed**

13	11	9	7		B	6	5	4	3	2	1

"Stores road"
Alongside left of Main Shed

Tank wagon 061197
(Esso 66132)
37412

37704
37517
37509

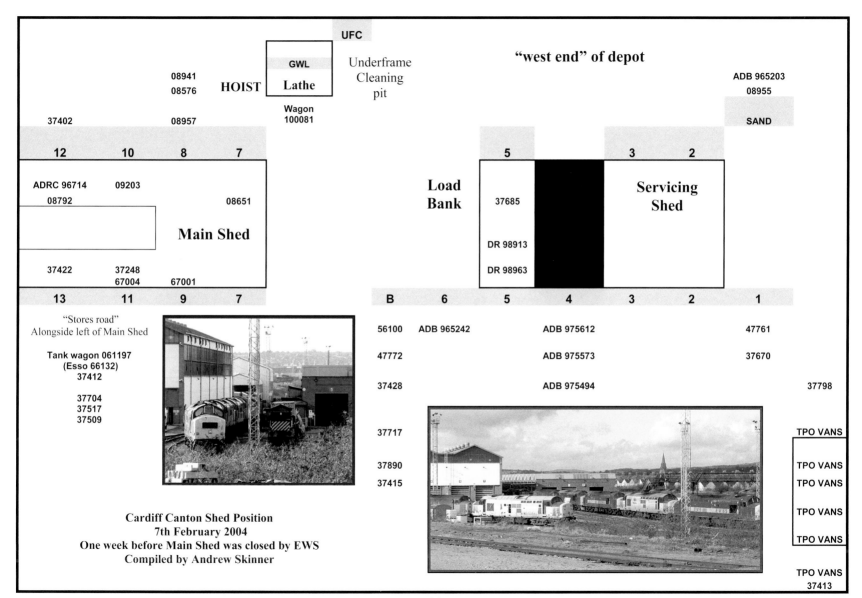

**Cardiff Canton Shed Position
7th February 2004
One week before Main Shed was closed by EWS
Compiled by Andrew Skinner**

B	6	5	4	3	2	1
56100	ADB 965242		ADB 975612			47761
47772			ADB 975573			37670
37428			ADB 975494			37798
37717						
37890						
37415						

TPO VANS

TPO VANS

TPO VANS

TPO VANS

TPO VANS

TPO VANS
37413

Plate 3

Western class locomotive D1043 "Western Duke" is seen during tyre turning on the original Canton wheel lathe located at the west end of the carriage shed adjacent to the DMU depot. "Westerns" continued to visit the depot for this work right up until the end of their use and even after this with the visit of 1013 & 1062 for such treatment in the summer of 1978 following preservation.
Condemned in April 1976, 1043 was cut up at Swindon works by February the following year, one of many of the class being dealt with in this way at the time.
Date 13th August 1973.
Photo Ian Walmsley

Plate 4

14th September 1973 and a week after display at Swindon works open day recently re-instated Hymek 7093 sits on the "Van Road" at the east end of the depot awaiting its next duty. This locomotive was finally withdrawn from Old Oak Common depot on November 26th 1974 before being dismantled by G Cohen Kettering in May of 1977, over 2 years after being condemned.
Photo Ian Walmsley

Plate 6 below
A classic view of the depot taken in 1965 less than 12 months after re-opening to Diesel traction. Examples of both types of Hydraulic locomotive allocated to Canton at the time can be seen stabled at the east end of the Main Shed occupying number 7, 9 and 13 roads.
Photo Ken Symons archive

Plate 5 above
A line of locomotives await attention on "C" road at the west end of the depot in November 1965. Canton class 14 "Teddybear" D9552 is flanked by Hymek D7098 and Canton class 47 D1964. D9552 would be transferred to Hull Darycoates by the end of 1966 where she would remain until withdrawal and sale to Stewarts & Lloyds in September 1968 with eventual cutting up in the autumn of 1980 whilst at Gretton Brook ironstone quarries Corby. D7098 went on to be a long term resident of the depot. Having been withdrawn as the last Canton based Hymek in December 1972, she remained on site until June 25th 1974 before being towed to Swindon works for cutting which finally took place in March the following year. Meanwhile, D1964 remains in use with Riviera Trains as "police liveried" 47829 having also carried the numbers 47264 and 47619 since July 1974.
Photo Brian Penney

13

Plate 7 below
A visitor to Canton. London Midland based class 45 "Peak" D121 is seen stabled outside the Servicing Shed waiting its next duty in July 1965. D121 was renumbered 45069 under the TOPS system and ended its working life at Toton depot in July 1986 before being towed to Vic Berry of Leicester for cutting which was completed by December 1988.
Photo Brian Penney

Plate 8 above
What was probably the first bogie change on a class 37 at Canton was undertaken on D6867 in December 1963.
In this view, the depot steam crane can be seen undertaking the lift at the top end of the depot site behind the DMU shed. This particular locomotive was less than 3 months old at the time so the change of bogies must have been associated with a warranty issue or perhaps derailment damage. D6867 became 37167 in March 1974 before being fitted with CP7 bogies and being re-numbered 37383 in January 1998 whilst allocated to EWS Eastleigh depot. Storage came in February 1999 before sale to Riviera Trains and finally to DRS in early 2002. 37383 is currently stored at LNWR Crewe not having seen service for over 7 years!
Photo Brian Penney

Plate 9
D1010 Western Campaigner is seen at the west end of the depot on August the 1st 1976 on what was probably her last visit to Canton whilst in service. Details of the visit are unknown but it is likely to have been for tyre turning. Withdrawn on 27th of February 1977 as one of the last of the class in traffic "Campaigner" remains in preservation on the West Somerset Railway although in the guise of D1035 "Western Yeoman". A more recent visit to Canton was made in December 1990, again for tyre turning but this time on the new lathe which would be situated just to the left of this view. **Photo Ian Walmsley**

Plate 11
Green liveried Hymek D7077 is found waiting departure from Canton in November 1965. New to Old Oak Common in December 1963, 7077 was allocated to Canton in August 1966 followed by a final transfer back to the London depot in January 1972.
Condemnation came at Worcester in July 1972 and a tow to Swindon works followed later that month. Cutting up took place by October 20th of the same year, less than 10 years since being delivered!
Photo Brian Penney

Plate 10
On May 12th 1987 a delegation from the Institution of Mechanical Engineers Railway Division visited Canton as part of their Summer Technical Meeting that was based in the area during that particular year. The depot put on a good show for the visitors. This included a line up of resplendent locomotives including 56037 "Richard Trevithick", 37901 "Mirrlees Pioneer", 08993 "Ashburnham" and 47484 "Isambard Kingdom Brunel" which had been repainted in GWR Green as part of the GWR 150 celebrations in 1985. In addition to this, the original "Richard Trevithick" was in steam outside the east end of the Main Shed in the area where this particular view was recorded. Quite a spread for 60 or so people!
Photo Brian Penney.

Plate 12 right

The Servicing Shed, or "SS" as it was commonly known, was located in part of the original depot buildings built in 1882. For the majority of its life, this part of the depot was manned for 24 hours a day throughout the year and dealt with a large number of locomotives from all over the network. Work carried out ranged from "FPX" fuel point examinations to "A" and "B" exams as well as minor running repairs.

In this view taken on July 7th 1986, Malcolm Ash and Alan Hill deal with a number of Canton based 37's that are parked on number 5 and 3 road, a common sight during the 1970's and 80's.

Plate 13 left

A line up of locomotives waiting their next duty is seen outside the east end of the servicing shed in April 1986. Both 37225 and 56054 were allocated to Canton at the time although they would be moving to other depots within a few months, 37225 to Immingham in June and 56054 to Toton in May.

Plate 14
The big freeze of January 1982 brought chaos to the area. The weekend of the 9th and 10th was particularly bad with complete suspension of services. One entry by supervisor Vernon Sheryn in the depot maintenance controllers log on Sunday the 10th referred to "33015 – Loco reported in area but not found yet"! Various members of staff were dispatched to wherever locomotives sat to cut coolant hoses and drain them down to prevent the power unit freezing up and cracking the engine block. This is a view of the west end of the depot at that time, nothing was moving!

Photo Ian Walmsley

Plate 15

An aerial view of the depot complex taken in June 1999 facing the east end of the facility. The Carriage Shed and DMU depot occupy the area to the left hand side whilst the white sided Main Shed and brick built Servicing Shed stand to the right of this. The Great Western mainline to Swansea and beyond passes alongside the Servicing Shed, the Lines to Barry, Penarth and ultimately the Vale of Glamorgan peel off to the left whilst the route which passes through Ninian Park station and on towards Radyr can be seen passing behind the DMU depot.

Photo Andrew Skinner

Plate 17 left
Carlisle Kingmoor allocated 25199 undergoes a change to No4 traction motor on the Jack Road on February 10th 1986. It was relatively unusual to carry out repairs of this nature on "foreign" locomotives, they would normally be sent "one journey" to their home depot for attention. No doubt, if 25199 had been based closer to Canton this would have been the case on this occasion as well.

25199 soldiered on for another 12 months before withdrawal in early 1987, although cutting by Vic Berry did not take place until 2 years later in April 1989.

Plate 16 right
25230, 08787 and 37163 line up on "C" road at the west end of the depot on February 5th 1986.

The class 25 had failed just north of Craven Arms at Marshbrook on January 31st whilst working the afternoon Manchester to Bristol parcels service and ended up at Canton. Loss of lubricating oil was diagnosed and repairs were quickly completed.

25230 lasted a further 5 months until withdrawal from service in June. Cutting came at Vic Berry's yard at the end of October 1987. 08787 lasted until February 1991 and was finally disposed of at CF Booth Rotherham in May 1994. 37163 would eventually become 37802 and end it's days in Spain following collision damage in January 2003 whilst on hire from EWS for Infrastructure duties. A building housing a new wheel lathe was to be built in this location 2 years later.

Plate 18 below
21st July 1988 and 37906 in partial "revised Railfreight" livery is seen parked alongside the new wheel lathe midway through a repaint having been kicked out of the Main Shed to make room for an upturn in repair work. The first of the 37/9's to be so treated, she was allocated to the Steel sub-Sector and remained in service under EWS until January 1999. At the time of writing, 37906 is part of the EWS heritage fleet and is currently located at the Severn Valley Railway.

Plate 19
Class 45's were relatively frequent visitors to Canton as a result of both passenger and freight workings in and out of the Midland and Eastern regions. In this view, 45013 is seen stabled outside the Main Shed in blizzard conditions in February 1985 when visits were becoming a lot less common. Withdrawal would come in April 1987 from Tinsley depot. Following a period of almost 7 years in store at March depot she was finally cut up by M.C Metal Processing at Glasgow works in February 1994.
Photo Ian Walmsley

Plate 20

20th July 1988. An overhead view of the east end of the Main Shed with 2 class 37's berthed in 11 road and 2 class 56's alongside in 13 road.

At this time, the majority of the depot's allocation consisted of these two classes with all apart from the 6 ETH fitted class 37/4 allocated to freight sector workings throughout the Western Region and beyond. The class 56 at the front, 56072, had only recently been transferred to Canton from Toton and was undergoing a C exam prior to entering the construction pool. Alongside is 37033 which was shortly to be despatched to Crewe works for refurbishment and re-numbering to 37719, the last 37 to be so treated.

Plate 21

A view of the supervisor's office in the Main Shed during September 1986. The board on the left contains the repair books and exam documentation belonging to the locomotives under repair at the time. These would be retained there until the repair was completed, the book being returned to the locomotive and the repair/exam paperwork to the documentation office for filing.

Plate 22

Although they had been occasional visitors to the depot since transfer to the Western Region, class 50's were diagrammed into Canton for servicing, particularly at night, on a regular basis in the mid 1980's. Often, up to four examples passed through the Servicing Shed on a typical night shift. It was important to get each one through and ready for service the next morning. One train in particular, the 1S61 Cardiff to Glasgow was diagrammed for a pair of 50's as far as Birmingham with one of them returning on 1V90 14.20 from Glasgow. In this view, 50035 and 50043 are seen side by side in the Servicing Shed undergoing exam in the early hours of September 6th 1986.

Plate 23

Canton based 47592 "County of Avon" is seen sandwiched between visiting 33008 "Eastleigh" and an unidentified class 31 on June 28th 1986. This class 47 ended its days in the EWS RES fleet based at Crewe diesel depot and was withdrawn in December 2000 before being despatched to Wigan Springs Branch for component recovery. Final cutting up was not completed until March 2003 by Sandbach Car & Commercial Dismantlers Ltd. Meanwhile, 33008 has recently entered preservation following storage at MoD Smalmstown under the ownership of Harry Needle Railroad Company having been withdrawn over 9 years ago!

Plate 25 below
The first locomotive to be dealt with on the new wheel lathe was Canton allocated Petroleum sector 47327 on June 3rd 1988. This example was withdrawn as life expired from Immingham in February 1993 ending its days during November of that year at Booths Rotherham. At the time of writing, this facility remains in use under the ownership of Pullman Rail Ltd.

Plate 24 above
The existing wheel lathe was approaching the end of its life by the mid 1980's and investment in a new one was authorised. This was a Hegenscheidt type 106 lathe that had a throughput that was no less than six times that of the original one. It was located at the west end of the Main Shed alongside the underframe cleaning pit and covering part of what was "C" road. In this view taken in November 1987 the structure of the building that would house the new facility is in the process of being erected.

Plate 26 right
Shortly after delivery from Crewe Works following refurbishment, ex 37288 now ETH 37/4 37427 sits outside the west end of the Main Shed on February 12th 1986. New to Canton in June 1965, apart from a few months in 1985, this locomotive was based here until September 1990. ETH fitment resulted in it initially working passenger diagrams throughout South Wales and the Cambrian Coast line along with 37426/428-431. At the time of writing 37427 remains in service with EWS based at Motherwell and has recently spent time back in South Wales working Cardiff – Rhymney passenger diagrams for Arriva Trains Wales.

Plate 27 left
The first "heavyweight" refurbished class 37 to be delivered to Canton was 37799, ex 37061. This view shows the locomotive parked at the east end of the Main Shed just after delivery on 29th of August 1986. This series of locomotives were ballasted up to 120 Tonnes to increase adhesion enabling them to replace pairs of un-refurbished 37's on MGR traffic for example. 37799 was one of 8 locomotives fitted with the GEC G564AZ alternator as fitted to 37905/906. At the time of writing this particular example remains in traffic on hire from EWS to GIF for infrastructure work in Spain and numbered L27.

Plate 28
Class 50's were regular visitors to the depot for tyre turning right up until the end of their use. 50010 is seen undergoing this treatment on the original wheel lathe in August 1987. "Monarch" was withdrawn in September 1988 and eventually cut up at Laira depot by Coopers Metals of Cardiff at the end of May 1992.

Major repairs

Plate 29 right

An example of the catastrophic damage that can occur. This is a view of the top of a piston fitted to 56038's power unit following cylinder head valve seat failure in August 1985. Apart from the damage to the cylinder head, piston and liner, smaller parts of this debris could then find themselves being sent to the turbocharger in the exhaust gas causing major damage to the turbine blades in the process.

Plate 30 left

June the 5th 1987 and 37230 has suffered major power unit damage following the failure of it's timing chain. In this view, one of the connecting rods is seen to have fractured at the big end putting "a leg out of bed" punching a hole in the engine block and damaging the crankshaft in the process. A visit to main works was needed for an overhauled power unit.

Plate 31

37128 viewed from above minus its power unit which was out for a generator change in August 1987. This was a repair that would normally be carried out at main works but on this occasion Canton took it on. Following a period in store 37128 was to be fitted with CP7 bogies as fitted to refurbished class 37's and re-numbered 37330 in September 1994.

A further two and a half years service followed before being withdrawn from service in February 1997. Interestingly, this locomotive was never officially withdrawn although it was finally cut up by T J Thompson Stockton in October 2001

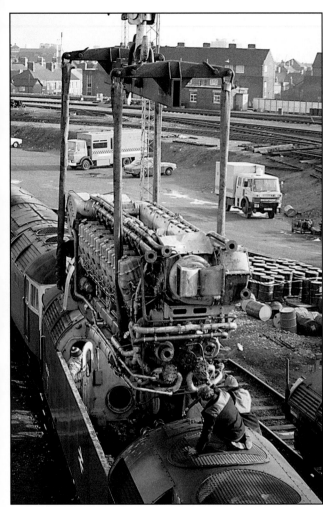

Plate 33
56054 suffered from repeated engine related problems throughout the second half of 1985. This manifested itself in failures of the pipework within the hydrostatic system that operated the radiator fan. It was finally established that this was due to excessive engine vibration when under load caused by a faulty vibration damper. In this long range view, it's power unit is seen in the process of re-installation following repair, using the depot's 75 Tonne breakdown crane. This was the only method available to do this until the new 50 Tonne overhead gantry was installed at the west end of the Main Shed a few years later. Date, 10th of January 1986.

Plate 32
The sheer size of the V16 Ruston RK3CT class 56 power unit is evident in this view as it is guided into 56054 by Dave Street. At this time it was not normal for a depot to take on this type of work, it would usually have been undertaken as an unclassified main works repair, but Canton was prepared to take on any job! Date 10th January 1986.

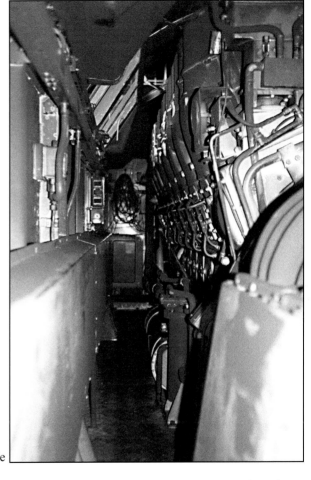

Plate 34

After being out of service since the middle of October 1985, 56054 is finally restarted by Technical Inspector Dave Owen along with fitters Roger Drake and Keith Allen on January 17th 1986.

This followed a complete strip down and rebuild of the power unit to cure the vibration problems mentioned on the previous page and also repair the damage caused by the excessive vibration such as worn main bearings and so on.

A few months after this repair was completed 56054 was transferred to Toton who were then able to take advantage of the high standard of work carried out! Withdrawal came in the summer of 2003 and at the time of writing "054" is dumped at the disused EWS Ferrybridge depot.

Plate 35 right

The restricted room available for class 56 maintenance is highlighted in this engine room view taken in January 1985. In fact, it was not possible to walk through the "A" side of the power unit due to it being blocked off at the free end making things even worse. This would not have been a problem if maintenance requirements were low but unfortunately this was generally not the case with the class 56! On this occasion, 56035 was 1 week off works attention when a cylinder head valve insert was "pulled" in service causing the sort of damage shown in plate 29 and resulting in the inside of the engine room being covered in soot in the process. 56035 was cut up at Wigan CRDC by June 2000.

Plate 36
One of the last class 45's to visit the depot, 45141 "Zephyr" waits its next turn of duty outside the Servicing Shed following an "A" Exam on May 26th 1988. At this stage in her career, 45141 was based at Tinsley for freight working although the presence of ETH meant use on some passenger work, particularly on summer Saturdays. For example May 21st saw her work the 16.20 York-Birmingham and only 5 days before withdrawal "141" was in charge of the 07.41 Leeds-Tenby on July 30th 1988. This particular locomotive ended its days at M.C Metal Processors in July 1992 but only after bring chaos to the WCML en route to Glasgow in March 1992 due to a roof panel from it, or 45128 that was also in the convoy, blowing off and coming into contact with the overhead electric line in the Warrington area.

Plate 38
Prior to Sectorisation, DMU's did make the occasional visit to the loco side of the depot if capacity allowed. In this August 1986 view Valley Lines set 334 is seen stabled in 8 road Main Shed undergoing ultrasonic axle testing following tyre turning. Alongside, 56048 undergoes a traction motor change on the Jack Road.

Plate 37 above
July 1988 and four class 37's are seen in the Main Shed undergoing attention. 37239 is parked in 7 road waiting release back to traffic following a D exam.
This example was loaned to the Southern region for crew training in early 1989 and was re-numbered 37332 in September 1994 following fitment of CP7 bogies. Withdrawal came at Old Oak Common in December 1998 where cutting up took place in the summer of 2000

Plate 39 right

Class 33's became regular visitors to Canton from June 1981 onwards when they took over from class 25's on the Crewe-Cardiff diagrams. This was followed by Cardiff-Portsmouth workings and into West Wales. By the mid 80's the depot was host to several of the class every day for servicing. In this 1987 view 33014 is seen with two other members of the class at the east end of the depot waiting its next working.

Photo Ian Walmsley

Plate 40 above

A wintry view taken from the depot footbridge at the east end of the depot in January 1987. A number of class 37's are parked up around the old water tower waiting service whilst a pair of 56's enter "the run" on their way onto the shed for maintenance. The number of locos sat on this road at any one time gave a rough guide to forthcoming workload. It could sometimes prove a challenge to keep this road clear on Friday nights in particular, especially if smaller depots in the area had decided to send across their "problems" for Canton to deal with over the weekend!

Plate 41 left

4th June 1987 and Bath Road allocated 37204, which was due classified repair at Crewe Works, is seen taking part in a double bogie change with Canton's 37197. In order to save time, a spare set of class 47 bogies were used as part of the procedure, probably the first and last class 47 bogied 37 to exist. The depot manager was not particularly impressed with the procedure, even though they did seem to fit pretty well !

Plate 42

The first of the new Foster Yeoman owned class 59's to visit Canton was 59003 for tyre turning on June 26th 1986 just before naming "Yeoman Highlander" at Merehead.

This locomotive was transferred to the German railway system in May 1997 and is now in use with UK based Heavy Haul Power numbered 259 003-2 as a part of private freight operations on the DB network.

Plate 43

January 1987 and 37696 sits on the depot load bank waiting test following repeated reports of "low power", the reason for which could not previously be established.

This facility was used on a regular basis to investigate faults such as this that could not be traced unless the locomotive was working under load, and also to set up and check power units following major repair or overhaul.

The procedure involved isolating the traction motors and connecting the main generator or alternator to a cooled resistor bank that absorbed the power generated by the locomotive throughout the power unit output range.

Plate 44

A visitor in the shape of Immingham based 31446 is seen outside 11 road with Canton's 37217 on November 20th 1985. It is likely that the 31 was waiting material to complete an unscheduled repair at the time, seeing them parked in the Main Shed area was not common. Renumbered 31546 in May 1990, this example was withdrawn 10 years later in November 1995 before being cut up at T.J Thompson Stockton-on-Tees in April 2003.

Plate 45

Class 08, 08994 "Gwendraeth", is seen here parked up at the west end of the Main Shed following completion of routine maintenance and a repaint in October 1994. This particular shunter was one of three that were modified with cut down cabs by Landore depot for working the Cwmmawr branch following withdrawal of the "cut down" Class 03's that previously worked this limited clearance route. 08994 was withdrawn in the summer of 2004 but is currently working in the Doncaster area having been stored at Canton until the end of October 2005.
Photo Andrew Skinner

Plate 46
A double bogie change for 56046 results in both the 50 Tonne hoist and 75 Tonne breakdown crane working in tandem during May 1991 just after re-allocation of the locomotive from Toton to Canton. 56046 was to remain in traffic until July 2002 and at the time of writing can be found languishing at Toton depot.
Photo Andrew Skinner

Plate 47
June 1995 and unusual visitors to the depot, 20087 and 20165 stand alongside 47212 outside the Servicing Shed. The class 20's were engaged in route learning in the area.
20165 was cut up by Michael Douglas Ltd Carlisle during December 2001 whilst 20087 lives on in private ownership.
47212 was allocated to Immingham at the time having been re-instated to traffic a few months earlier following a period in store. She was to remain in traffic with Freightliner until February 2003 before being cut up at the LNWR depot Crewe during March 2004.
Photo Andrew Skinner

Plate 48
From late 1996 Canton took on the role of overhauling Travelling Post Office vehicles as part of the EWS Royal Mail contract. In this view a TPO is seen on the Jack Road undergoing a bogie change. Another TPO vehicle can be seen in 9 road whilst in the foreground on 8 road is an 80 Tonne steel carrying (BDA) wagon, the depot having also started general repairs on these wagons for EWS at the time.
The date is October 1997 and not a locomotive in sight!
Photo Andrew Skinner

Plate 49
Canton often took on sub-contract work on other owners locomotives. In this July 1992 view Industrial shunter 08113 is seen undergoing tyre turning on the new wheel lathe. At the time this locomotive was owned and operated by Powell Duffryn Coal Preparation Gwaun-Cae-Gurwen having been withdrawn from Canton in March 1984.
08113 remains in service as part of RMS Locotec's hire fleet.
Photo Andrew Skinner

Plate 50
The 50 Tonne hoist in action again and a double power unit swap is taking place on Immingham based Petroleum sector locomotives 37891 and 892.
The fact that Canton was one of the only depot facilities able to carry out this work meant that it was able to take on contracts such as this. 37891 was to remain in service until October 2000 having been hired out by EWS for French infrastructure work for over 12 months. This locomotive is currently dumped in Tyne yard and unlikely to see active service again. 37892 was withdrawn from EWS Toton in January 2000 and is currently dumped at Old Oak Common depot.
Photo Andrew Skinner

Plate 52 below
Canton began to receive the full fleet of 30 class 67's for use primarily in Royal Mail traffic at the start of 2000. In this view taken in April 2000, brand new 67011 is parked up against withdrawn 37904 engaged in crew training activities having arrived at Newport Docks on board the "M V Stellanova" only a few weeks before.
Following closure of the depot the class 67's were transferred to Toton. However, since EWS lost the Royal Mail contract, class 67 fleet utilisation has inevitably dropped and use on freight duties has become more common as a consequence of this.

Plate 51 above
The class 66 has provided the majority of EWS' motive power since introduction of the 250 strong fleet during 1998-2000. Canton had an allocation of approximately 50 of these locomotives up to closure, replacing life expired class 37's and 56's on coal and steel workings throughout the area. 66111 is pictured in April 2000 parked on "B" road at the east end of the depot along with a number of stored class 37's. This includes Regional Railways liveried 37414 that had been removed from traffic a few weeks earlier.

Canton today

Plate 53 right

Pullman Rail Ltd purchased Canton from EWS in January 2005 and needed to make a number of changes to the depot layout to suit their bogie overhaul business. A view of the Main Shed looking down 7 road from the east end taken in September 2005 reveals that the platforms have been removed and several pits filled in. Here, a selection of bogies fitted to passenger rolling stock can be seen undergoing overhaul in the area once occupied by 9 road. The tracks in 7 road remain in situ for wheelset storage.

Photo Steve Morris
courtesy of Pullman Rail Ltd

Plate 54 left

Following sale of the depot to Pullman Rail a number of EWS locomotives remained on site for several months. The last mainline example, 37509, was cut up there at the end of August 2005. In this view, withdrawn Transrail liveried 08792/955/651 are seen dumped on number 1 road at the east end of what was the Servicing Shed, unlikely to see active service again. The water tower remains in situ in the background. These shunters eventually left Canton by road transport in October 2005. See plate 39 for a comparative view taken some 18 years earlier.

Photo Steve Morris courtesy of Pullman Rail Ltd

The People !

For the majority of its life the Main Shed was manned over 3 shifts Monday to Friday and on various shifts over the weekend depending on workload and in particular on Sunday morning and night. The Servicing Shed provided a 24 hour service and was open every day of the year except Christmas Day.

Staffing varied depending on the size of the depot's allocation and associated workload. The management structure also varied during the 40 years of operation with major changes in the early 90's following privatisation and then the takeover of the operation by EWS. However, as an example, during the late 1980's with an allocation of in the order of 160 locomotives there was a compliment of 104 skilled fitting staff along with 35 semi skilled staff/fitters mates/labourers, all working over 3 Shifts, 0600-1400, 1400-2200 and 2200-0600 one week at a time. Management was provided in the form of one D and C grade supervisor in the Main Shed, a D grade Servicing Shed supervisor and D grade maintenance controller who was responsible for liaising with regional control regarding the maintenance requirements of day to day arrivals at the depot and ensuring that locomotives were available to meet service needs.

Plate 57 above
L-R Ron Mourissi, Ken King, Fay Spencer, Gaynor Crocker, Dave Barney and Depot Engineer Mike Etwall.
Date, 22nd June 1979. **Photo Ian Walmsley**

Plate 55 left
In the days before the introduction of computerised record keeping, the "Docs Office" played an important part in the running of the depot. Things look a bit hectic for Paul Fairfax on this particular day in November 1988!
Photo Ian Walmsley

Plate 56 right
Alan Hill and Dave Petigan take a break in the Servicing Shed.
30th July 1987

There was also a Shift Engineer available for the majority of the time who was responsible for the overall operation of the depot on a shift by shift basis. This meant setting priorities, ensuring that availability and reliability targets were met, releasing locomotives from major exams and so on. Finally, the whole operation was managed by the Traction Maintenance Engineer who in turn reported to the Depot Engineer who also had responsibility for the DMU maintenance facility as well.

As with any organisation, the people were Cantons main asset and I was fortunate to work with a great number of experienced staff of all grades during my time there. There is not room to mention everybody but a selection of photographs follow of some of the maintenance team, several of whom have sadly passed away over recent years. I hope these will bring back a few memories to those who were employed at the depot during its life.

Plate 58 above
Bill Webb, Charlie White, Reg Richards and Huw Jones pose with replacement nameplates for Canton allocated 47088/089/090 on January 18th 1979
Photo Ian Walmsley

Plate 59 left
Maintenance controller Bill Howells takes a break in April 1986. This job could often be particularly hectic, it was the Maintenance controllers job to ensure that the right locomotives were available for service in the right place at the right time!

Plate 60 right
Fitters mate Paul Keedwell assists with a cylinder head replacement on a class 56 power unit in December 1985.

Plate 61 left
Canton held an open day on the 6th of July 1985 as part of the GWR 150 celebrations. In this view, the organiser Ian Walmsley (7th from the left) along with Gaynor Cornock, Brett Cornock, Richard Skinner, Doug Cooper, Valerie Bowen, Wendy Walmsley, Paul Fairfax, Graham Binding, and Alan Jones pose in front of one of the exhibits during the evening before the event.
Photo Ian Walmsley collection

Plate 62 below left
Wheel lathe operator John Armstrong is seen alongside the original lathe waiting the arrival of his next loco during the summer of 1987.

Plate 63 below
C shift Main Shed supervisor Max Hillier and Shift Engineer Mike Bates stand in front of the Main Shed shop floor office on the 4th of April 1989

Plate 64
From late 1996 Canton took on the role of overhauling Travelling Post Office vehicles. In recognition of the hard work put in by a lot of people in turning their hand to new skills, C W Pennel MBE (EWS Business Manager—Royal Mail) and staff of the Royal Mail TPO section at Willesden came to Canton to meet the staff concerned.
Date September 1997.
Photo Andrew Skinner

Plate 65 above
Each shift had a "breakdown gang" made up of volunteers. Normal duties involved attending derailments and other such incidents but occasionally other jobs required the use of the 75 Tonne crane allocated to the depot such as power unit lifts or assistance with bogie swaps between locomotives.
In this view, B shift gang are seen alongside the crane and tool van waiting to replace a class 56 power unit. Date, January 1986.

Plate 68 right
Huwel Lewis repairing
the bufferbeam pipework
on 47615 following a
collision with a herd of
cows near Swindon.
Date 19th August 1986

Plate 66 above
Dave Barney, Brian Penney and Depot Engineer
Mike Etwell alongside Canton allocated 47254
on May 4th 1978. This particular locomotive
remains in service as Virgin Thunderbird 57309.
Photo Ian Walmsley

Plate 67 right
Mike Casey (first left), Director of Mechanical
and Electrical Engineering BRB with members
of C shift and the Managing Director of Ruston
Diesels are seen alongside 37905 "Vulcan
Enterprise" during its naming ceremony on
number 9 road Main Shed.
Date 3rd February 1987.

Plate 70 left
C shift fitters Martin Fink and Martin Thomas occupying a vacant class 47 cab during the morning breakfast break! Date, 8th January 1986.

Plate 71 below
37235 was the first of the class to receive the new Trainload Coal livery at the depot. This particular locomotive was allocated to the Speedlink Coal Network (SCN) sub-Sector and in this view painters Don White and Mike Edgeworth can be seen with Traction Maintenance Engineer Ken King at the west end of the Main Shed just after completion of the painting.
This was done in association with naming "The Coal Merchants Association of Scotland" in Aberdeen on November 3rd 1987, the "SCN" sector fleet certainly travelled far and wide!
Date, 29th October 1987.

Plate 69 below
April 1986. Derek Parry and Phil Nethercot assist with the fitting of the nameplates to recently refurbished 37426 just prior to naming "Y Lein Fach/Vale Of Rheidol at Aberystwyth station on May 5th 1986.

Special occasions

Canton was responsible for the preparation of locomotives for special events. This could have been for working the Royal Train, or for locomotive naming for example.

The standard of work carried out by the depot was extremely high. In fact, following the allocation of the 37/4's in 1986 we seemed to spend a lot of time undertaking this sort of work. Each of the 37/4's along with a number of the freight variants were named during 1986-88 and several Royal trains ran. Add to this the naming of several class 56's and repaints into new liveries following Sectorisation and it is easy to see why we utilised several staff almost full time to concentrate on this work during this period!

Plate 72 above
To celebrate the movement of the one millionth Tonne of steel by rail from Cardiff Rod Mill, 37229 was named "Cardiff Rod Mill" on May 23rd 1984.
This view taken just after the naming ceremony at the Rod Mill shows the locomotive waiting departure from the works sidings.
Withdrawn from service with EWS in December 1999, 37229 is now owned by DRS and in regular service again.
Photo Ian Walmsley

Plate 73 left
During the GWR 150 celebrations held in 1985 several locomotives received repaints into "GWR" livery.
This included 47079, "George Jackson Churchward". Here she can be seen undergoing the repaint in 7 road Main Shed on July 20th 1985 just prior to being fitted with brass name and number plates. This particular locomotive remains in service with Freightliner Ltd as 57009.

Plate 74 right

Having originally been allocated the name "City Of Hereford" on paper, 47615 stands outside the east end of the Main Shed having just been prepared for naming "Caerphilly Castle/Castell Caerffili" instead. The ceremony took place at Caerphilly station two days later on April 30th 1985, another naming associated with the GWR 150 celebrations during 1985.

New to Bristol Bath Road as D1629 in February 1966, this particular 47 also carried TOPS number 47252 whilst allocated to Canton in March 1972 and finally 47747 as part of the EWS RES fleet based at Crewe Diesel depot in April 1994.

Withdrawn in early 2004, 47747 is currently dumped at EWS Millerhill depot unlikely to work again.

Photo Ian Walmsley

Plate 75 left

An immaculate 56053 has just arrived back at Canton following naming "Sir Morgannwg Ganol/County Of Mid Glamorgan" at Porth station on March 17th 1986.

New to Toton in December 1978, 56053 was first allocated to Canton during the period September 1984 to September 1991. During a second spell at the depot in 1997 she received fire damage which was rectified by Brush Traction Loughborough during December of that year. 56053 was taken out of service in July 1999, at the time of writing can be found dumped at Healey Mills depot.

Photo Ian Walmsley

Plate 77 below
Double headed Class 37's took over the majority of Royal Train workings in the area from classes 25 and 47 with the arrival of the ETH fitted examples in 1986.
In this view, 37430 is coupled up to 37426 awaiting departure from the depot to work a "Royal" over the Cambrian Coast Line. This caused a last minute panic for the author having arrived at the depot for the day shift to learn that 426 had failed on its trial run to Newport during the night! Luckily it was a relatively straightforward job to rectify the problem but a few anxious hours were had up until both locomotives left the depot!
Date July 14th 1986
Photo Ian Walmsley

Plate 76 above
For several years class 25's were responsible for Royal Train workings, particularly over routes such as the Central Wales or Cambrian Coast lines. An unidentified member of the class waits to leave the depot on May 5th 1978 to work to Crewe on such a service having been prepared for the job at Canton. The additional cable in the area of the blanked off front end doors will be used to allow communication between the locomotive crew and those on board the train.
Photo Ian Walmsley

Plate 78

New to Canton as D6999 in August 1965 and renumbered 37299 under TOPS in early 1974, 37426 was one of the first refurbished 37's to be allocated to the depot in February 1986 as one of 6 ETH fitted examples.

In this view she can be seen on May 1st 1986 catching the evening sun outside 8 road Main Shed having just been prepared for naming "Y Lein Fach/Vale of Rheidol". The ceremony took place at Aberystwyth station on the 5th May. Unofficially named "Mt Vesuvius" and "Macsaveus" during spells allocated to Tinsley and Thornaby in the early 1990's, 37426 is currently dumped at the closed EWS Crewe Diesel depot.

Plate 79 above
Having just been released following repaint into "red stripe" Railfreight livery, 37250 is pictured parked at the station end of the Van Road on September 9th 1987. This particular 37 was repainted in preparation for naming "Coal Merchants Association of Scotland". However, it was then decided to name 37235 instead (see plate 71) so "250" remained nameless.

Plate 80 top right
09017 was the first of its class to be allocated to Canton, specifically to work the Severn Tunnel emergency train. Re-numbered 97806 it spent most of its time based at Sudbrook pumping station. Parked at the west end of the Main Shed, 97806 is seen here waiting movement to Sudbrook following an E exam and repaint into a unique livery. After undertaking this role for several years this shunter reverted to its normal number and general duties. At the time of writing 09017 remains in service with EWS and is located in South Wales once again.

Plate 81 right
Following repair and repaint, NCB owned class 08, D3014, is seen waiting transfer back to Merthyr Vale colliery in March 1986. Sold to the NCB from Eastleigh depot in October 1972 this locomotive passed into preservation following closure of the colliery at the end of August 1989 and can now be found operating on the Dart Valley Railway.

Plate 82

47237 was a long term Canton locomotive having been delivered there new in November 1965 as D1914 and remaining until transfer to Tinsley in July 1987. In this particular view she is seen under storm clouds following collision damage repairs and repaint on October 7th 1986. 47237 remained in traffic with EWS until February 1999 and was then stored until sold to DRS in September 2002. A further period in store followed until overhaul at Springburn works Glasgow and eventual entry to service with DRS in March 2003.

Plate 83

A rare view of a locomotive inside Cathays wagon repair shop. 37414 was present for naming "Cathays C&W Works" on March 18th 1993 whilst based at Crewe Diesel depot and allocated to North Wales Coast passenger diagrams.

Delivered new to Canton via a short loan spell on the Eastern Region in July 1965 as D6987 and then 37287, this locomotive was never allocated to Canton following refurbishment. Withdrawal came from Toton in March 2000 and even though a spell was spent in the component recovery shop at Wigan Springs Branch, "414" was eventually saved for preservation by the Class 37 Locomotive Group in September 2005 and can currently be found at the Weardale railway.

Photo Andrew Skinner

Plate 84 left

30th of July August 1987 and Don White puts the finishing touches to 37429 in preparation for naming "Eisteddfod Genedlaethol" at Portmadoc station on August the 4th. "429" also carried the name "Sir Dyfed/County of Dyfed" between April and July of the same year!

Plate 85 right

Half of the Canton 37/4 fleet line up outside the west end of the Servicing Shed waiting to be serviced prior to working a Royal Train during the summer of 1990.

37431 was available as standby locomotive whilst 37430 & 37427 worked the train itself.

Photo Andrew Skinner

Plate 86

April 13th 1986. Locomotive hauled services were suspended over Barmouth Bridge to Barmouth and Pwllheli for over 5 years in the 1980's due to damage caused to the 1866 wooden structure by the Torado marine worm.

In this view from the cab, 37427 heads the first locomotive hauled train across the bridge following repair to its structure, in multiple with 37426. On arrival at Barmouth, 37427 was named "Bont y Bermo", a name carried until April 1993 prior to fitting to 37402 in early 1994.

Following this reopening, Canton 37/4's took over Cambrian Coast passenger duties and in particular the new London Euston to Pwllheli service. **Photo BR**

Bont Y Bermo

37427

Plate 87

37220 was delivered new to Canton as D6920 in January 1964. In this view she is seen in recently applied Railfreight Petroleum livery leaving the Tytherington branch at Yate conveying invited guests to the Murco distribution terminal on the Westerleigh branch to be named "Westerleigh" on June 12th 1990.

Withdrawn from service by EWS in January 2000, 37220 was cut up by EMR at Kingsbury during November 2005

Plate 88

56044 was named "Cardiff Canton" by Boilersmith George Wright who passed away shortly afterwards following a brave battle with cancer. In this view, the locomotive concerned is seen parked outside the Main Shed following the naming ceremony on the 9th of August 1991. Following George's death, small commemorative brass plaques were added underneath each nameplate as well as with the 3rd nameplate that was displayed in the depot entrance. These nameplates are currently carried by withdrawn 37422 located at EWS Toton depot.

Taken out of service at Immingham in December 2000, 56044 still remains dumped there some 5 years later.

Photo Andrew Skinner

Plate 89

Resplendent in Railfreight Coal livery, refurbished class 37 37800 "Glo Cymru" sits outside 9 road Main Shed with 37698 "Coedbach" following exam and repaint during the summer of 1991. Previously numbered 37143, 37800 was involved in a major derailment near Marine Colliery Ebbw Vale on January 29th 1975 which resulted in it falling down an embankment and being badly damaged. Recovery proved so difficult that it was not completed until six months later in August! 37698 can currently be found withdrawn at Margam depot having been among the last batch of mainline locomotives to leave Canton following closure. 37800 remains in service in Spain on hire from EWS to GIF for infrastructure work and numbered L33.

Photo Andrew Skinner

Plate 91 left

37430 was named "Cwmbran" in recognition of the opening of Cwmbran station on May the 11th 1986. As can be seen in this view, a good crowd turned out for the event which was also broadcast by the local media. 37430 can now be found waiting its fate at EWS Motherwell depot, over 5 years after being withdrawn from service.

Plate 92 below

Canton, Summer 1992. First built class 37 D6700 was allocated to Canton between November 1988 and October 1992. During this time she was fitted with CP7 bogies and numbered 37350 having been repainted in green livery at Stratford depot. This locomotive was donated by EWS to the National Railway Museum in August 2000.
Photo Andrew Skinner

Plate 90

An addition to the livery of a number of Canton class 37's was "Selwyn the sheep" which was applied by a Barry based driver. An example is seen here applied to 37230 in late 1985.

Prototypes

Canton was entrusted with the maintenance of a number of prototype locomotives during its history. The sole class 53, 1200 "Falcon" was allocated to the depot between October 1972 and May 1973. However, visits to Canton were not very frequent. One was recorded between the 17th and 18th March 1973 for load bank testing. She also paid a visit to the Main Shed between the 11th and 22nd May 1974 for a wheelset change whilst allocated to Ebbw Junction shed Newport where Falcon was based for the majority of her time in South Wales.

Withdrawal came on the 5th of October 1975 as a result of a traction motor bearing collapse that had occurred in June of the same year. Cutting came shortly afterwards at the yard of John Cashmore Newport, the process being completed by 15th April 1976.

The 47/9 and 37/9 locomotives could be considered "full time" depot prototypes. 47901 was a test bed for the Ruston

12RK3ACT power unit/Brush alternator combination that was eventually used in the class 58 build. Originally numbered 47046, this locomotive was rebuilt as 47601 during 1975 to act as a test bed for the class 56 Ruston 16RK3CT power unit and Brush alternator. Further conversion to 47901 came during 1978/79 before being allocated to Canton in June 1980 where the locomotive was put to use on steel traffic and MGR coal workings between Newport docks and Didcot power station. There then followed a spell allocated to Bristol Bath Road between October 1982 and November 1987 where 47901 was outbased at Westbury for Mendip stone traffic.

During May 1986, "901" paid a visit to Toton depot for a piston change. This was at the request of Ruston Diesels due to the fact that the class 58's that were running with essentially the same power unit were suffering numerous piston failures at the time, whereas 47901 was not. It was hoped that examination of these pistons would go some way to explaining why this was the case.

Plate 93
Pictured in its final livery, Railfreight Construction, 47901 is seen parked at the east end of the Servicing Shed waiting transfer back to Westbury following attention in the summer of 1989. Within a few months this particular prototype would be withdrawn from service.
Photo Andrew Skinner

The locomotive was then run-in at Doncaster works before returning to service. One interesting story associated with the return to traffic following this attention was the sight of 47901arriving at Doncaster station for crew change at the head of a southbound oil train. When questioned by a member of the WR HQ locomotive section who just happened to be on the platform at the time, the Immingham driver admitted that he could not understand why this particular 47 was "more lively" than others! Given that traincrew had to have specific traction knowledge to drive 47901, how it ended up in this position was a mystery.

Use in Mendip stone traffic then continued following re-allocation back to Canton in November 1987 and the locomotive ended its days allocated to the Railfreight Construction sub-Sector.

47901 was a popular locomotive with traincrew and was relatively reliable, particularly given its "one off" status. In the authors opinion the beginning of the end came following a visit to BRML Doncaster for an F exam in December 1987. Years of hard work to get the power unit "just right" was undone in an instant and the locomotive was returned in a worse condition than it had left the depot! Reliability reduced and this resulted in several other visits to Doncaster, none of which seemed to make any difference, right up until withdrawal. 47901 was taken out of service in March 1990 and eventually cut up by M.C. Metal Processing Glasgow during March 1992.

Plate 95
Complete with faded paintwork, "Falcon" is pictured at the yard of J Cashmore in Newport just prior to being cut up early in 1976, something that would be completed by April of that year.
Photo Brett Cornock

Plate 94
1200, "Falcon" seen ticking over waiting its next turn of duty at Newport Ebbw Junction depot. This view was recorded on December 10th 1972 during the short period of 7 months or so when the locomotive was allocated to Canton.
Photo Jeff Clements UK Wayfarer.co.uk

37901 to 37906 were test beds for a new power unit that was being aimed at a proposed medium power class 38 Diesel locomotive to eventually replace the class 37, something that never actually came about.

37901 to 904 were fitted with a Mirrlees MB 275T power unit whilst 905-906 had the newly developed Ruston RK270T installed.

37901-904 power units were coupled up to a Brush BA1005A alternator in common with the majority of other refurbished class 37's whilst 905-906 utilised the GEC G564AZ alternator, Ruston Diesels being owned by GEC at the time. The remainder of the locomotive was overhauled to the same standard as other refurbished class 37's being released by Crewe works with modified sanding gear, redesigned control cubicles, increased fuel capacity, electromagnetic radiator fan clutches, a complete re-wire etc.

In addition, all six locomotives were ballasted up to 120 Tonnes as was the case with the 37/7 variant as well as being fitted with Gloster Saro silencers.

They were delivered to Canton during the second half of 1986 and immediately put to work on a variety of freight duties including Llanwern-Port Talbot iron ore in multiple and various Steel flows including those to Dee Marsh and the Midlands.

From a maintenance point of view, experience with both types was good, with much improved engine room access. However, as with any non standard design, provision of spares became an issue and when class 37 withdrawals commenced the 37/9's were removed from service during 1995-98 as major repairs became necessary.

Plate 96
37906 was the first "37/9" to be painted in the revised Railfreight livery. Pictured on August 2nd 1988 at the west end of the depot complex, this is a view of the locomotive running down to the Servicing Shed prior to being released back into traffic.

It is difficult to establish which version of 37/9 was the most successful but of course Mirrlees won the contract to power the class 60, although with a different power unit. From a reliability point of view, all six locomotives performed well.

A snapshot of the performance of Canton's locomotive allocation early in 1988 (table 5) demonstrates the importance of the class 37 as a whole. It shows the complete fleet in a good light with the side only being let down by 37430 which had suffered two electrical faults during the period in question. At the time, a "casualty" was defined as a delay of five minutes or more to a passenger service (ten minutes for freight) caused by a technical issue associated with the locomotive in question.

Class	Reliability – Miles per Casualty		Availability %	
	Target	Actual	Target	Actual
37/0	20,000	67,000	76	75
37/4	15,000	8,500	67	74
37/5	20,000	Infinity	82	82
37/7	20,000	20,000	78	77
37/9	20,000	Infinity	67	83
47	17,500	35,500	80	73
56	9,000	7,300	71	59

Table 5
Canton locomotive performance - 4 week period ending 2nd January 1988

Plate 97
August 1984 and 47901 is pictured under gathering storm clouds with a train of empty PGA hoppers in Westbury Down Yard.
A trip to ARC Whatley quarry followed prior to returning with a loaded service bound for West Drayton.
At this time "901" was based at Bristol Bath Road depot and had just undergone an E exam and repaint.

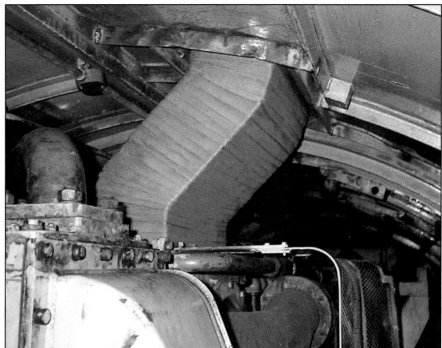

Plate 98 above
One of the early problems experienced with the 37/9's surrounded failures of the silencer casings. One novel way around this was to dispense with the silencer altogether! 37906 was treated in this way and the result is pictured above, custom built, straight from the turbocharger to atmosphere!
Photo Andrew Skinner

Plate 99 left
The simple layout of the Mirrlees MB275T power unit is evident in this view of 37902 with the roof removed for silencer repairs. The coolant rail runs along the left hand side with the exhaust manifold situated underneath. At the far end is the turbocharger, next comes the intercooler and charge air chamber running off this along the right hand side. Fuel pipes run up behind the charge air chamber to individual fuel injectors that pass through the top of each rocker cover.

Incidents & withdrawals

Derailment and collision damage to any fleet of locomotives is an inevitable part of railway operation although thankfully not a regular occurrence. Canton was one of a handful of depots on the network to have a high capacity recovery crane allocated to it. This was manned by a breakdown gang made up of volunteers from each shift and ready to attend any incident at short notice. In later years, minor derailments were dealt with using a "Road Rail" Bruff vehicle equipped with hydraulic jacks and re-railing beams.

The first Canton allocated Diesel locomotive casualties were class 47 D1671 "Thor" and 37 D6983 which were written off following a collision at Bridgend station on the 19th of December 1965. Only a handful of locomotives were ever cut up at the depot. These included 47111 in March 1987 following collision damage in January 1986, 37273 in May 1993 after derailment in January 1991, 47198 in July 1994 following fire damage in March 1989 and 56001/016 along with 37031/080 as life expired during the summer of 1997. Finally 37509, again life expired, was cut up in August 2005, some 15 months after the depot had closed!

The following views depict the type of incidents that arose, the damage that could be inflicted and in some cases demonstrates the lack of protection available to the traincrew in cases of front end collision.

Plate 100
An early mishap for Canton based D1022 "Western Sentinel" occurred in the summer of 1964 when she split the points at the far west end of the depot complex as can be seen in this view. Minor collision damage was to spell the end for this particular locomotive in January 1977 during the final run down of the fleet. **Photo Brian Penney**

Plate 101 right

New to Canton as D6946 in October 1964, 37246 was based at Tinsley when photographed outside the Main Shed in July 1985. Having suffered front end collision damage, her power unit was swapped with another example of the class at Canton prior to being despatched to Crewe works for refurbishment.

Returning to Canton in February 1986 as 37698, this particular locomotive would eventually be named "Coedbach" in September 1988.

37698 was regularly transferred in and out of store for use in Sandite application duties at the end of the 1990's prior to final withdrawal in April 2002. See also plate 89

Plate 102 left

A routine job for the Canton breakdown gang on January 9th 1986. In this view the depot's resident 75 Tonne breakdown crane can be seen re-railing Bath Road based 47144 that had run through catch points near to Severn Tunnel Junction Yard. The class 37 in the background that worked the breakdown train on this particular day is 37182. This particular 37 would shortly become 37670 and spend many years working China Clay traffic in Cornwall operating from Laira depot.

Withdrawn from Railfreight Distribution traffic based at Tinsley in the summer of 1997, 47144 was broken up by Booth Roe Metals Rotherham 12 months later.

Plate 103

The first Diesel locomotive to be broken up at Canton was 47111. Allocated to the depot for several periods during the 1970's and 80's, 47111 was based at Crewe on January 19th 1986 when involved in a collision with a class 104 DMU in Preston station. At the time, Canton was in need of a spare set of class 47 bogies to act as a float for a bogie overhaul programme that was due to commence, so the complete locomotive was towed to the depot. The bogies were removed for this purpose, the power unit and good cab despatched to Crewe works for further use. In this view taken on June 4th 1986, the locomotive body is seen being removed from it's bogies to be placed on sleepers for cutting up by depot staff, something that would take until October 1987 to complete!

Plate 104

One of the most serious incidents involving the collision of two passenger trains in the Cardiff area occurred in platform 2 of Cardiff Central station on December 21st 1985. The 18.15 Cardiff to Manchester service headed by 33024 ran into the rear of the 18.10 departure for Portsmouth at just after 6pm. The Portsmouth service had just completed the run round movement and the tail lamp had not been replaced at the time of the collision due to the station staff dealing with attaching the locomotive at the time. The driver of the Manchester bound service, H. R Bullar of Hereford, was fortunate to avoid serious injury having sustained minor cuts and bruises. four passengers also suffered minor injuries as a result.

Plate 105

33024 was towed to Canton the following day and in this view she can be seen being prepared, under the watchful eye of Shift Engineer Keith Meyrick in 12 road Main Shed, for onward transfer to Eastleigh depot and further examination.

The locomotive was finally towed from Canton on January 21st 1986 and withdrawn on February 17th at Eastleigh depot as a result of the damage seen here.

Cutting was carried out by Eastleigh depot staff during May 1986.

Plate 106
August 1991 and not having connected the automatic air brake pipe between the locomotive and a 3000 Tonne train of iron ore, it was little wonder that 60034 could not stop its train when departing Port Talbot iron ore terminal with the locomotive straight air brake alone on the approach to the signal protecting the main line! The train ran through the catch points and derailed with the 102 Tonne capacity iron ore tippler wagons piling up behind it in the process. Recovery took two days to complete, not helped by the fact that a 3000 psi oxygen main was running under the site!
In this view, on call Engineer Mike Bates discusses the next move with other members of the local area management team.
Photo Andrew Skinner

Plate 107
47589 was working to Cardiff from Crewe during September 1985 when it was in collision with the jib of a JCB that had been left fouling the line! Luckily the driver saw the approaching danger and managed to vacate his seat in time. In this view the Canton based locomotive is seen under the original hoist at the west end of the depot waiting transfer to Crewe works for attention.

Plate 108 below right
A view of 47589's cab following the collision. This particular locomotive remains in service as Virgin Thunderbird 57302.

Plate 109 below
47282 suffered severe front end damage on April 27th 1986 whilst engaged on engineering works in the Micheldever area. Following a short visit to Canton for removal of several components she was towed to Crewe works in June 1986 and condemned. Cutting up came at C F Booth Rotherham by October 1989.

Plate 111 below
Once back at Canton the locomotive body was grounded and finally cut up by Gwent Demolition of Margam during May 1993. On arrival at the depot it was discovered that the copper air pipe work and traction motor cables from within the locomotive had been "liberated" by persons unknown during its time overhanging an embankment whilst supported by little more than three telegraph poles!

37273 had been numbered 37306 following the introduction of the TOPS numbering scheme in 1974 and been part of a small number of locomotives dedicated to triple headed class 37 iron ore workings between Port Talbot and Llanwern until the arrival of the class 56's in 1979.
Photo Andrew Skinner

Plate 110 above
On January 6th 1991 Petroleum sector 37273 was involved in a derailment at Gulf Branch Junction between Milford Haven and Haverfordwest whilst hauling a tank train. As can be seen in this view taken shortly afterwards, the damage was severe and resulted in the locomotive being condemned.

Due to the position in which it was lying, re railing did not take place until April 28th 1991. This involved a double lift using both the Canton and Old Oak Common 75 Tonne cranes with additional assistance from the Margam breakdown gang. The whole operation was completed in under 8 hours. The locomotive was then towed back to Canton at low speed.
Photo Andrew Skinner

Plate 112.   July 1991 and Metals sector 37903 is pictured at Margam depot having suffered front end collision damage and a "drooped nose "as a result. This Mirrlees prototype was to remain in traffic with EWS until December 1998 and ended its days in October 2005 when cut up at the disused EWS Crewe Diesel depot by local contractors.

Photo Andrew Skinner

Plate 113

37799, Canton's first "heavyweight" class 37, suffered a derailment in early September 1986 on its first run in revenue earning service following refurbishment. In this view taken in Margam yard, preparations are being made to re-rail the locomotive. At the time of the mishap 37799 had been running with 56035 coupled dead in train as insurance during commissioning, something that clearly did not help prevent this particular problem occurring!

Photo Ian Walmsley

Plate 114

56001, the pioneer class 56 ended its days at Canton, having been allocated to the depot during the later part of the 1980's as part of the Construction sector pool working out of Westbury. Withdrawal came in May 1991 whilst based at EWS Stewarts Lane depot. Following a period of store at Willesden yard she was towed to Canton for component recovery as part of the consist of a Dover to Pengam Freightliner in May 1994. In this view taken in March 1997 the locomotive can be seen parked on the stores road just prior to being cut up by M.R.J Phillips of Llanelli during May.

Photo Andrew Skinner

The final mainline locomotive to leave Canton was 37509. Dumped at the depot when withdrawn from sandite duties with EWS in 2002, "509" was finally cut up on site during the summer of 2005.
Previously numbered 37093, this class 37 was based on the Eastern region until refurbishment in 1986 and was in fact only ever allocated to Canton for a few weeks following this treatment. Interestingly, as 37093 she was repainted in "Police livery" for a filming session in the North East during the summer of 1985 whilst based at Gateshead depot.

In this view, 37509 can be seen in the final stages of being dismantled at the far west end of the depot on August 24th 2005 whilst a Swansea bound HST passes by.
Photo Paul Fairfax

Plate 115 above
The second and final class 47 to be broken up at Canton was 47198. This particular locomotive caught fire at Basingstoke whilst working a Longport to Fawley tank train on March 22nd 1989. Withdrawn on April 20th she was towed to Canton and dumped on the stores road, where pictured in this view taken during August 1990.
The end came some four years later when the locomotive was cut up on site by M.R.J Phillips of Llanelli in July 1994.

Canton Diesel locomotive duties

During its 40 year history, locomotives allocated to Canton were responsible for a number of workings covering both passenger and freight duties. A major change came during the mid to late 1980's when sectorisation resulted in Canton primarily becoming a freight depot following the ending (apart from several class 37/4's) of passenger locomotive maintenance under Transrail and then EWS.

A summary of typical duties covered by Canton allocated locomotives over the years follows:

Shunters – Class 08/09

At its peak, Canton had an allocation of nearly 50 shunters. As would be expected, these were used locally and in particular by the NCB within the numerous collieries that existed in the South Wales Valleys up until the mid 80's. The introduction of MGR and Block Train working along with a general reduction in Railfreight and demise of the South Wales coal industry resulted in a significant reduction in allocation over the years. Towards the end of its life a shunter allocation remained at Canton with a shift to on-site maintenance by a dedicated team of staff at various locations throughout the region.

Class 14

A total of 56 class 14's were built at Swindon works during the early 1960's. The initial idea was for them to take over duties such as trip working, yard shunting and transfer freights previously undertaken by Pannier Tanks throughout the Western Region. However the Beeching cuts of the late 60's resulted in a major reduction in demand for this form of traction.

Plate 117
Class 14 "Teddybear" D9509 seen parked at Newport Godfrey Road whilst in the process of being delivered to Canton in September 1964.
This particular locomotive was loaned to Ebbw Junction depot between October 1964 and May 1965 for crew training. In December 1970, 9509 along with 9519 was the last class 14 to leave Canton. Cutting up came within a few weeks after just over 6 years service !.
Photo G H Hunt. Colour Rail image DE2016

The situation was made worse by poor reliability of the class. Canton received its first allocation of class 14's in July 1964 with the arrival of D9501 straight from Swindon works. At one stage almost half of the fleet were based at the depot but this was short lived. Rationalisation of yards and closure of many branch lines finally resulted in there being no need for the class 14 and as early as 1966 many examples were placed in store! Canton lost its allocation at the end of 1968 although the last examples to leave the depot did not do so until 8th December 1970 when long term stored 9509 & 9519 were towed to Kettering and cut up by G Cohen Limited the following February.

Interestingly, as late as April 1970, and following withdrawal from service, 9519 and 9535 had been used as part of major track replacement work between Craven Arms and Hereford, and 9535 had been used as the depot pilot in August of the same year.

By April 1969 the class 14 ceased to officially exist on British Railways books. Following a short period of use on the Eastern Region, the majority of this fleet were sold in almost new condition to the NCB and British Steel where they gave many more years good service. Five of the class (9505/15/34/48/49) were exported overseas and no less than 19 examples remain in preservation today.

Class 25

Class 25's were initially allocated to Canton in the early 1970's taking over some of the duties previously undertaken by Hymek class 35's that had recently been withdrawn from service. In addition to this, from 1975 onwards they replaced the DMU's that covered Cardiff - Crewe passenger diagrams. These workings remained in the hands of class 25's up until May 1981 when class 33's took over with ETH stock. They were also used for a short time on freight workings to Ebbw Vale steel works but this was not a success.

Never particularly popular with Canton traincrew, direct association with the depot was short lived and by the late 1970's the allocation had ended. However, this class remained a frequent visitor to the depot for servicing and repair up until their withdrawal, primarily as a result working into Severn Tunnel Junction on inter regional freight duties.

Class 35 "Hymek"

Canton had a long association with the "Hymek" Diesel Hydraulics. D7022 was the first mainline diesel to be allocated to the depot at the end of February 1962 and during their life no less than 76 of the 101strong fleet were allocated to the depot at one time or another.

These locomotives were responsible for a mixture of passenger and freight workings throughout the region. One such duty, the Cardiff – Portsmouth passenger diagrams were a particular stronghold for the class.

The non standard nature of the class resulted in it seeing a premature end with the majority not seeing much more than 10 years service. The last major repair on a "Hymek" at the depot was the fitting of a replacement transmission to Old Oak Common allocated 7031 on November 27th 1972. The transmission had in fact been delivered to Canton for use in 7090 a few months earlier but the decision was made to withdraw the locomotive instead.

Plate 118

25063 enters Church Stretton station at the head of a Cardiff to Crewe working on February 22nd 1977.

One of a number of 25's allocated to Canton for workings such as this at the time, 25063 was transferred to Crewe in November of the same year. Withdrawal came three years later although disposal did not take place until March 1983 at Swindon works.

Canton lost its Hymek allocation in December 1972 with 7093 being transferred away to Bristol Bath Road and finally Old Oak Common where she gave a few more months service. The withdrawal of 7098 on the 19th of the same month ended the depots ten year direct association with Diesel Hydraulic locomotives. The last Canton based Hymek to leave the depot did not do so until the 25th of June 1974 when long term stored 7098 was towed to Swindon works for cutting. Finally, following two years in store, 7076/7096 were towed across to the depot from Bristol Bath Road during July 1974 for tyre turning prior to their use by BR Research.

Class 37

Probably the most well known locomotive type to be allocated to Canton, the class 37 was associated with the depot throughout its life. At one stage over 100 examples were based there.

Not surprisingly, this class was utilised primarily on freight workings, particularly those associated with the Coal and Steel industry in the area. Regular passenger duties did not commence until early 1986 although occasional workings as substitutes for class 25 and 47's did occur in the years before this. However, following the allocation of six 37/4's after refurbishment, they took over the Cardiff to Bristol leg of several Portsmouth diagrams as well as workings in West Wales and the Cambrian and Cardiff to Manchester & Liverpool routes to name a few. Passenger workings remained until the very end with several peak hour Rhymney Valley diagrams still 37/4 hauled right up until the closure of the depot. Following sectorisation, Canton's 37's were allocated to a number of dedicated pools covering the Steel, Petroleum, Coal and Departmental sub-Sectors along with a Regional Railways pool to cover the passenger workings mentioned above.

Plate 119
July 1966 and Canton based Hymek D7085 is pictured running through Newport High Street station with a rake of empty coal wagons. New to Canton in June 1963, this example was to spend most of its life allocated between Canton and Old Oak Common depots before being condemned at the London depot in October 1972. A trip to Swindon works followed almost immediately where cutting up was complete by November 10th, less than a month after withdrawal.
Photo Bruce Nathan. Colour Rail image DE1777

Class 46

A relatively short association with the depot for the class 46 started in 1975 but was over by May 1977 with the last of the class transferred away to Laira.

A primary duty for the class involved working the Cardiff to Newcastle passenger diagrams up until the introduction of ETH stock, along with a number of inter regional freight workings.

Class 47

Another class with a long association with Canton. The depot had an allocation of 47's right from the official opening in October 1964 with over 60 of the class based there at one time in its history.

Workings included passenger and freight duties throughout the region (although never regular visitors to the Welsh valleys) and inter regional diagrams covering the North East/South Wales corridor and Welsh Marches. A number of slow speed fitted ("SSF") 47's were also based at the depot for working MGR trains through Aberthaw power station. This necessitated a locomotive change at the power station from the double headed class 37's working each train. The need for this ended with the arrival of refurbished "SSF" fitted 37's in 1986. The class was also involved in South Wales to London Paddington workings following withdrawal of the Class 52's and prior to the introduction of HST operation.

The depot lost its allocation of class 47's following the formation of Transrail in 1994 although the class remained frequent visitors right until the end.

Plate 120
One of the original Western Region named class 47's, 47077 "North Star" is pictured at Hereford on an inter regional working destined for the West Country in February 1977. New to Landore as D1661 in February 1965, "North Star" was allocated to Canton between October 1976 and July 1984. Further re-numbering to 47613 came in May 1984 with fitment of electric train heating, followed by 47840 at the end of 1989 when modified with extended range fuel tanks.

At the time of writing, Porterbrook owned 47840 remains in service with GB Railfreight having spent the summer of 2005 employed on stock movement duties between Paddington and Old Oak Common for First Great Western.

Class 52 "Western"

The "Western" Diesel Hydraulics played a large part in the early life of Canton with the initial allocation of D1012 "Western Firebrand" in November 1962.

Primary duties were regional passenger workings in the South and West Wales to London corridor. At some stage during their life no less than 47 out of the 74 members of the class were allocated to the depot. Canton retained an allocation of "Western's" until April 1966 when the entire remaining allocation of 14 locomotives was transferred to Laira. However, the class continued to visit the depot right up until the end in early 1977, primarily due to the fact that tyre turning was carried out there. This also resulted in occasional use on Paddington to West Wales duties right up until the summer of 1976 due to the fact that Canton drivers retained traction knowledge in order to get locos to and from the depot's wheel lathe. In addition to the above, having lost the majority of their mainline passenger work by the mid 1970's, appearances on secondary freight duties in South Wales continued right up to 1976.

Plate 121
Whilst Canton based Western's spent most of their time working to and from South Wales and London and into West Wales, D1052 "Western Viceroy" is seen off the beaten track at Blatchbridge Junction near Frome working the 17.30 Paddington to Plymouth in June 1964. This particular locomotive was allocated to Canton from new in January 1964 and remained there until transfer to Landore in February 1965. Withdrawn from Laira depot on October 6th 1975, "Viceroy" was finally cut up at Swindon Works during April 1976.
Photo P.A Fry. Colour Rail image DE2258

Class 56

Canton received its first class 56 allocation in July 1979 with the arrival of 56036 for driver and depot training. Having been built as a dedicated freight locomotive it is not surprising that passenger duties did not feature in the diagrams covered by the class!

Initial workings included the Port Talbot – Llanwern iron ore diagrams to replace triple headed class 37's. This was the first time that regular double heading of the class had been seen. Other early workings included Margam – Trostre/Velindre steel, Landarcy to Aberthaw/Llanwern oil, Llanwern to Shotton steel, import coal workings from Newport to Didcot as well as Freightliner services between Danygraig and Stratford as well as Pengam to Glasgow as far as Crewe.

An increase in allocation came with the use of the class on Mendip stone workings and in particular with the transfer of the Bristol Bath Road allocation to Canton in 1987 as a result of Railfreight pulling out of Bristol. From October 1987, three class 56 pools were established at Canton namely (number allocated) Steel (3), Construction (15) and Petroleum (3). The workings covered included the most arduous seen by the class such as the 4,400 Tonne Merehead to Acton "Jumbo" train which conveyed aggregate in rakes of 43 102T bogie hoppers for onward distribution throughout the South East via feeder services. This may have gone some way to explain the poor reliability experienced during this period and the resulting investment in GM class 59 traction by Foster Yeoman and ARC to handle a large proportion of their services.

Rationalisation of the fleet allocation following privatisation resulted in Canton's allocation of 56's increasing to 45 in 1994 with an even wider range of duties being covered. The class 56 certainly accounted for a large proportion of the depots workload throughout their association with it.

Class 60

Plate 122
56041 and 56052 head an empty iron ore working through Marshfield between Newport and Cardiff on June 1st 1986. Having been the first double headed class 56 diagrams in the country when introduced in late 1979, these duties were transferred to double headed refurbished "heavyweight" class 37's and finally class 60's in following years. 56041 was withdrawn from service with EWS in February 2003 and is currently dumped at Healey Mills depot. 56052 has been dumped at EWS Immingham depot since April 1999. Neither are likely to work again.

Another dedicated freight locomotive, the financial case for manufacturing the class 60 was made by terminating the class 37 refurbishment programme at 135 locomotives. The first allocation to Canton was made in 1991 with the arrival of 60010 in January of that year.

A large proportion of the fleet was allocated to Canton during their life with a wide range of duties covering various parts of the country where they replaced class 37's in many cases.

Class 66

Whilst it could be argued that this was the beginning of the end for Canton, the introduction of a more reliable form of traction to replace first and second generation locomotives was essential to EWS. They had to turn to General Motors for this and the result was a build of 250 class 66 locomotives. These would eventually replace classes 37, 56 and even several class 60's operated by the company, and of course the workload that was generated by them.

Canton was involved with every member of the class (apart from 001) due to them being shipped to the UK via Newport docks and Canton staff being responsible for initial inspection following off loading from the ship. The first allocation came in July 1998 with the transfer of 66001 to the depot for training. Over the next few years and right up until closure, a large number of the fleet were associated with the depot although changes in diagramming and maintenance policy resulted in visits only being necessary for major exams.

Plate 123
An example of how far away workings took new generation locomotives from their home depot. 66055 approaches Winsford station on October 18th 2002 on a rake of 90T bogie ballast wagons.

Plate 124
67005 seen approaching Shrewsbury station on a northbound Royal Mail working during July 2000. This particular example of the class is now one of the class 67's allocated to Royal train workings.

Class 67

Another "GM" locomotive although built in Spain under sub-contract to Alstom, the class 67 was introduced during 1999/2000 primarily for use in Royal Mail traffic operated by EWS. The complete class was allocated to Canton following delivery and worked Royal Mail traffic throughout the country, only returning home for major exam or repair. The loss of this contract in 2003 effectively made the class redundant and the resulting loss of this traffic and maintenance workload was probably the final straw for Canton.

Other allocations

During its life, several other allocations were made. Perhaps the most notable was that of Class 53 locomotive "Falcon". Following various trials on BR under the ownership of Brush Electrical Machines in the late 1960's, Falcon was taken into BR stock in December 1970. Initially allocated to Bristol Bath Road this locomotive was allocated to Canton between October 1972 and May 1973 for working between Newport docks and Llanwern.

Another interesting allocation was the loan of class 20's 20179 and 20201 from the Scottish region between the 7th and 24th of May 1979 for trials in South Wales MGR traffic. These trials were not a success and apart from the occasional visit to the depot for servicing, class 20's were never a regular sight at Canton.

Plate 125 right

As a result of problems with the power operated doors fitted to the class 155 DMU's based at Canton from 1988 onwards, the complete fleet was withdrawn from service on December 16th 1988 for modifications. Apart from class 156's being drafted in to take their place, ETH class 37's took up several of their diagrams on the North and West route to Manchester and Liverpool.

In this view, drafted in from Eastfield depot, 37407 approaches Church Stretton working the 13.15 Cardiff to Liverpool service on July 29th 1989.

Plate 126 above

On loan to Canton, 20179 and 20201 are seen stabled on number 1 road at the east end of the Servicing Shed on May 21st 1979, a few days before transfer back to the Scottish Region.
Photo Ian Walmsley

Plate 129 right

The first working for Cantons fleet of six ETH fitted 37's that arrived at the depot in early 1986 took place on February 12th. 37427 did the honours less than 24 hours after delivery from Crewe Works.

In this view the locomotive is seen waiting to depart from platform 1 at Cardiff Central on the 14.05 working to Bristol Temple Meads, something that went without incident.

Almost 20 years later, 37427 would still be working passenger trains in and out of Cardiff during 2005!

Plate 130 left

Many years before to the start of class 37 passenger workings on Rhymney Valley services, occasional DMU substitutions took place using a spare class 37/4 along with whatever rolling stock was available at the time! In this view taken on March 5th 1987, 37426 is seen starting up in the carriage shed coupled to several air conditioned MK2 coaches to form the 17.05 service to Trehebert. No doubt, the regular commuters had a more comfortable ride up the valley than usual! This was repeated several times during this period, a class 50 being utilised on at least one occasion

Plate 131
Class 60's took over iron ore workings soon after being delivered to Canton. In this view, 60037 "Helvellyn" is seen heading a laden service past Canton No 2 inlet ground frame during 1993. This particular locomotive had spent March 1992 to March 1993 under repair at March and Toton depots. Perhaps it was still suffering with some sort of problem judging by the fact that Technical Inspector Dave Owen travelling in the back cab seems to be taking a great deal of interest in the rear bogie of the locomotive!   **Photo Andrew Skinner**

Plate 132 below
37695 approaches Aberdare station during April 1989 on a loaded MGR service for Aberthaw power station. The coal had been extracted at Tower colliery near Hirwaun which at the time of writing is the last deep mine operating in Wales.

New to Canton in the summer of 1963 as D6857 and later 37157, this locomotive was one of a batch of class 37's transferred to Scotland in the mid 1960's only to return to South Wales in early 1986 as refurbished 37695.

Plate 133 above
A scene typical of the Welsh valleys until the late 1980's. July 1st 1986 and recently refurbished 37697 (ex 37243) and unrefurbished example 37244 head a rake of empty MGR hoppers towards Taff Merthyr colliery having just passed close to Deep Navigation pit. Double heading on these diagrams would soon end with the arrival of the first "heavyweight" refurbished 37's that could handle these workings single handed.

Sunk in 1924 by Powell Duffryn, Taff Merthyr once employed 1,380 men underground with a further 195 on the surface and was producing 600,000 tons of steam coal a year by 1936. Taff Merthyr mine was closed in 1992 and workings along the branch from Nelson are now a memory.

Plate 134 below
Class 37 number 6974 is seen here shunting empty wagons into Canton Brickyard alongside the depot.

Delivered from the English Electric Co Vulcan Foundry works to Canton in April 1965, this locomotive was one of the first to be refurbished and fitted with ETH in the summer of 1985 having been renumbered from 37274 to 37402 and transferred from Canton to Eastfield depot Glasgow in the process. She then spent over 8 years working in Scotland prior to being transferred south to Crewe in October 1993. A further period of passenger use on the North Wales Coast then followed and eventually a transfer back to Canton in November 2001 for use on Rhymney Valley line passenger services came following a period in store.

At the time of writing 37402 is dumped at EWS Toton for component recovery having recently donated its bogies to 37411, see plate 151, to keep this particular example in traffic.

Photo Ian Walmsley

Plate 135 above
By the time the above view was recorded on April 12th 1988, single "heavyweight" 37's had completely taken over MGR workings to Aberthaw power station. Here, 37896 is seen at the head of a train being loaded at Deep Navigation colliery Treharris using a mechanical digger.

Deep Navigation was sunk in 1873 and was first known as Harris Navigation. At the time it was the deepest mine in the coal industry at 2,280 feet with 10 miles of underground railways! Bought by David Davies of Llandinam it was renamed Ocean colliery and reputed to produce the best steam coal in the country. The "Ocean" name was still being used by railway operating staff in the 1980's even though it had been named Deep Navigation following nationalisation in 1947. The pit closed in 1991 shortly before nearby Taff Merthyr also ceased production.

Plate 128 below
When first introduced, the iron ore workings between Port Talbot docks and Llanwern steel works were the heaviest freight services operating on the UK rail network, grossing over 3000 Tonnes.
These diagrams were operated by triple headed class 37's based at Canton and Landore. In this view taken in August 1978, 37301/298/304 pass through Cardiff Central station with a loaded train bound for Llanwern. 37301 would eventually be refurbished and ETH fitted for use in Scotland as 37412. She would eventually spend several years back at Canton in the mid 1990's before being withdrawn from service at the depot in January 2001 following spells based at Toton and Crewe. At the time of writing. 37412 is dumped at Margam depot.

Plate 127 above
Mirrlees engined prototypes 37903 and 37902 are pictured at Llanwern steel works coupled to their train of JUA/JTA iron ore tippler wagons having just completed discharging their load.
Double headed "heavyweight" refurbished class 37's were introduced to these workings during 1988. This particular photograph dates from April 1992 during a period in which the 37/9 fleet were used on these diagrams. Both locomotives were part of the FMCK Railfreight metals sector at the time and wear the "Triple Grey" Railfreight livery with Steel sub-Sector markings.
Photo Andrew Skinner

Plate 135
56032 "County of South Glamorgan/Sir de Morgannwg" is seen storming through Westbury station on a rake of empty 51T PGA hoppers bound for Foster Yeoman Merehead quarry on July 5th 1988. At this time, 56032 was part of the Construction sub-Sector and spent a large proportion of its time outbased at Westbury for aggregate workings alongside the Foster Yeoman owned class 59's. At the time of writing, this locomotive can be found working in France on infrastructure construction duties on hire from EWS to Fertis.

Photo Colin Webb

Plate 138 left
37371 and 37258 run through the centre road at Cardiff Central station on an empty Petroleum working from Theale to Milford Haven on April 6th 1990.

37371 was previously numbered 37147 prior to fitting with re-geared CP7 bogies in October 1988. Withdrawal came in November 1999 following a collision with 90033 at Rugby. 37371 was cut up at Wigan CRDC during June 2001.

37258, based at Thornaby at the time of this photograph, would eventually be fitted with CP7 bogies and numbered 37384 in October 1998. Following a spell in sandite service during 1999, 37384 was withdrawn in September 2000 and following several years in store at Brush Traction Ltd was eventually cut up at EMR Kingsbury at the end of 2005.   **Photo Colin Webb**

Plate 137 left
Canton hired a number of class 08's to the NCB. In this view, 08488 is seen at Cwm colliery waiting attention to an electrical fault on November 20th 1985. An NCB owned 0-4-0 shunter can be seen in the background.

Plate 139 previous page below left
An interesting Petroleum sector service was the daily
BP Llandarcy to Isle of Grain bitumen working.
In this view, Canton based 60033 heads the loaded
service through Pilning station on August 9th 1991,
6 months after being delivered new to the depot.

Plate 140 right
September 1989 and the unlikely sight of an ETH 37
pairing on a freight train! 37428 and 37430 stand at
Jersey Marine on a train of Cawood containers full of
domestic coal for export to Ireland from Ellesmere
Port. The re-introduction of class 155 DMU's
following modifications had resulted in a reduction
in traffic for these locomotives and they occasionally
found themselves used on freight diagrams during this
period.
Photo Andrew Skinner

Plate 141 left
A Speedlink coal network (SCN) working is pictured waiting
to leave the branch at Pantyffynnon with Canton based 37212
at the head of a rake of loaded PFA's and HEA's originating
from Gwaun-Cae-Gurwen during April 1992.
Locomotives allocated to this sub-Sector worked throughout
the country moving domestic coal to several locations, Canton
being the central maintenance location for all traction used in
this traffic.
37212 was transferred to Glasgow Eastfield depot the
following month and ended its working life in the summer of
1999 when withdrawn from service at EWS Eastleigh depot.
The locomotive was finally cut up there by Raxstar almost 5
years later during January 2004.
Photo Andrew Skinner

Plate 143 next page top right
A rare view of a military working at Cwmbargoed on the branch from Ystrad Mynach on the Rhymney Valley line. 60054 stands at the head of a train of light tanks and ambulances that have just been loaded following army exercises in the Brecon area.

New to Canton in May 1991, "Charles Babbage" was in fact allocated to Toton at the time of this picture on October 30th 1998. This particular location was more accustomed to dealing with coal traffic for Aberthaw power station with fuel had been dug from several open cast mines in the area.

Photo Andrew Skinner

Plate 144 next page bottom right
37372 in Railfreight "red stripe" livery at Machen quarry waiting for it's ballast train to be loaded before working back to Newport East Usk yard in July 1990.

New to Canton as D6859 in June 1963, this locomotive was renumbered 37159 in March 1974 before becoming 37372 after fitment of CP7 bogies in June 1988. Withdrawn from service in October 2001, this locomotive can currently be found dumped at EWS Motherwell depot waiting a call to the breakers yard.

Photo Andrew Skinner

Plate 142
An unusual working for Metals Sector locomotive 37902, seen at Tondu heading a rake of empty MEA's up the Garw valley to Pontycymmer. At this time there was a market for low grade coal and the tips of the former mines in the Garw valley were being reclaimed. Date June 1994.

The 37/9's were popular with drivers once they had got accustomed to the time they took to take power compared to the standard locomotives of this type. This resulted in several cases of these prototypes being booked for "low power" when first introduced earning them the nickname "slug" as a result.

Photo Andrew Skinner

Plate 145 above

Summer 1992 and 56040 & 56032 are pictured at Port Talbot iron ore terminal loading another consignment for delivery to Llanwern steel works.

The River Severn was not dredged sufficiently for iron ore carrying ships to dock at Llanwern, hence the need to unload at the deep water terminal at Port Talbot docks. The ore delivered here was split between Llanwern and Port Talbot steel works with that required for Llanwern being conveyed there in trains of 102T iron ore tipplers comprising 30 JUA/JTA wagons giving a trailing load of over 3000T.

Photo Andrew Skinner

Plate 147 below

Canton had an allocation of ETH fitted class 47's for passenger duties up until sectorisation and the depot becoming a freight sponsored facility. In this view taken on July 7th 1986, Canton based 47624 heads a southbound Intercity service through Great Bridgeford just north of Stafford.

New to Canton in the spring of 1965, D1673 (47087) was named "Cyclops" and became one of the original Western Region named 47's when based at Bristol Bath Road in 1966. This locomotive spent the first 26 years of its life based on the Western Region allocated to Canton, Bath Road and Old Oak Common at various times during this period. Transferred to Crewe Diesel depot in May 1991, 47624 was renamed "Saint Andrew" when used in Rail Express Systems service with EWS. Withdrawal came in November 1998 and at the time of writing this locomotive can be found at CF Booth Rotherham having been purchased for preservation.

Plate 146 above

A regular class 37 diagram during the 1990's was a summer dated service between Cardiff/Bristol and Weymouth. In the summer of 1993 this involved an 09.30 departure from Temple Meads returning at 16.30. These trains were made up of 6 coaches with a Crewe based 37/4 booked as motive power. Substitutions with Canton based freight sector 37's and 47's were common as seen in this view of 37191 approaching Berkely Marsh on August 5th 1993.

37191 was part of the Civil Engineers pool at the time and spent most of this particular week working the diagram. Withdrawn in February 1999 at EWS Toton, this locomotive was dismantled at Wigan CRDC in January 2001.

Photo Colin Webb

Plate 148 right

Another summer dated passenger service was a Cardiff to Fishguard return which ran for several years from 2000 onwards.

This service was diagrammed for one of the 37/4's that were based at Canton for working several peak hour Rhymney Valley line services, during it's layover between peak hours. Departing Cardiff Central at 10.35 this service ran via the Swansea avoiding line before returning at 13.35 from Fishguard, understandably this was a popular train with rail enthusiasts!

In this view, 37419 has just completed the run round at Fishguard Harbour and is being attached to the return working to Cardiff on August 1st 2002. At the time of writing, this particular locomotive has just completed a spell working to Rhymney and back on a daily basis, these diagrams having ended on December 10th 2005.

Plate 149 left

37417 was withdrawn in November 1999 and stored at Canton, Barry wagon works and finally Allied Steel and Wire Castle Works Cardiff in February 2002. The closure of the ASW works in August of 2002 resulted in 37417 being towed to Canton and a decision was taken to return the locomotive to service. At the time of this view, taken at the back of the DMU depot at Canton on February 7th 2004, 37417 was one of several 37/4's based at Canton for Rhymney Valley services.

This locomotive is one of a handful of 37's still operated by EWS and is based at Motherwell depot.

Plate 150
A step back in time. Canton based D6990 is pictured at the head of a rake of Mineral wagons at Ystrad Mynach in April 1968.
Renumbered 37290 in 1974, this locomotive remained allocated to either Canton or Swansea Landore until being refurbished in 1985 and transferred to the
Scottish Region for passenger duties operating out of Glasgow Eastfield.
Photo Brian R Arman. Colour Rail image 2300

Plate 151

A testament to the success of the English Electric type 3 class 37. Same locomotive, same location as the previous photograph and even wearing the same livery but over 36 years later! 37411(ex D6990/37290) enters Ystrad Mynach station on September the 10th 2005 working a Rhymney to Cardiff Central service, over 40 years after this locomotive had been delivered new to Canton.

Plate 154 next page
A classic view of a pair of class 37's doing battle with the elements! 37206 and an unidentified member of the class are seen on snowplough duties on February 12th 1979. The location is Dowlais Top, at the end of the freight only branch from Nelson to Cwm Bargoed and Dowlais, right at the top of the South Wales Valleys.
Photo Ian Walmsley

Plate 152 above
66125 runs through Bridgend station on a rake of MGR coal hoppers on August 1st 2002. Delivered via Newport Docks on board the "M V Gajah Borneo" on June 17th 1999, this locomotive was initially allocated to Toton and forms part of the 250 strong fleet of class 66's that is the backbone of the EWS fleet.

Plate 153 right
The Canton based class 67's travelled far and wide. Pictured undertaking a "non Royal Mail" duty due to the loss of this traffic during the previous year, 67004 is seen entering Valley station on Anglesey with a crew training run on March 30th 2004. Canton would close its doors to locomotive maintenance within two months of this view being recorded and the entire fleet of 67's transferred to Toton.
Photo Pat Webb

Plate 155
Llanbradach station on July 1st 1986. 37278 leads recently refurbished 37503 (ex 37017) down the Rhymney valley on a loaded MGR from Penallta colliery bound for Aberthaw power station. Penallta was situated at Hengoed with rail access just north of Ystrad Mynach station.
Opened by Powell Duffryn in 1906, this colliery employed no less than 3,200 miners at one stage! Penallta was closed on November 1st 1991.

Left
Sunset over the west end
of Canton Diesel depot

Right
Found mounted on the
notice board within the
wheel lathe building
a week before the Main
Shed closed on February
14th 2004. R.I.P
Photo Andrew Skinner

Back cover
Canton based Hymek 7070 sits outside the Servicing Shed on the 16th
of May 1971. Withdrawn in January 1972 after less than 9 years in
service, 7070 was then re-instated and stored several times without
actually carrying out much useful work. She was finally condemned at
Old Oak Common on September 8th 1972 and rapidly cut up at Swindon
works within 4 weeks.
Photo Ian Walmsley

Published by

Ty Mawr Publications

ISBN 0-9552354-0-5

9 780955 235405

£12.95